SELECTED POEMS

FARRAR STRAUS GIROUX

ROBERT PINSKY

SELECTED POEMS

NEW YORK

Farrar, Straus and Giroux
18 West 18th Street, New York 10011

Copyright © 2011 by Robert Pinsky
All rights reserved
Distributed in Canada by D&M Publishers, Inc.
Printed in the United States of America
First edition, 2011

Library of Congress Cataloging-in-Publication Data
Pinsky, Robert.
    [Poems. Selections]
    Selected poems / Robert Pinsky.— 1st ed.
    p. cm.
    ISBN 978-0-374-25860-3 (alk. paper)
    I. Title.

PS3566.I54 A6 2011
811'.54—dc22

                                        2010044668

Designed and composed by Quemadura

www.fsgbooks.com

10 9 8 7 6 5 4 3 2 1

CONTENTS

FROM

JERSEY RAIN

(2000)

FROM

THE WANT BONE

(1990)

FROM

GULF MUSIC

2007

RHYME

Air an instrument of the tongue,
The tongue an instrument
Of the body, the body
An instrument of spirit,
The spirit a being of the air.

A bird the medium of its song.
A song a world, a containment
Like a hotel room, ready
For us guests who inherit
Our compartment of time there.

In the Cornell box, among
Ephemera as its element,
The preserved bird—a study
In spontaneous elegy, the parrot
Art, mortal in its cornered sphere.

The room a stanza rung
In a laddered filament
Clambered by all the unsteady
Chambered voices that share it,
Each reciting *I too was here*—

In a room, a rhyme, a song.
In the box, in books: each element
An instrument, the body
Still straining to parrot
The spirit, a being of air.

IF THE DEAD CAME BACK

What if the dead came back not only
In the shape of your skull your mouth your hands
The voice inside your mouth the voice inside
Your skull the words in your ears the work in your hands,
What if they came back not only in surnames
Nicknames, names of dead settlement shtetl pueblo

Not only in cities fabled or condemned also countless dead
Peoples languages pantheons stupidities arts,
As we too in turn come back not only occulted
In legends like the conquerors' guilty whisperings about
Little People or Old Ones and not only in Indian angles
Of the cowboy's eyes and cheeks the Dakota molecules

Of his body and acquired antibodies, and in the lymphatic
Marshes where your little reed boat floats inches
Above the mud of oblivion O foundling in legends
The dead who know the future require a blood offering
Or your one hand accuses the other both lacking any
Sacrifice for the engendering appetites of the dead.

GULF MUSIC

Mallah walla tella bella. Trah mah trah-la, la-la-la,
Mah la belle. Ippa Fano wanna bella, wella-wah.

The hurricane of September 8, 1900 devastated
Galveston, Texas. Some 8,000 people died.

The Pearl City almost obliterated. Still the worst natural
Calamity in American history, Woh mallah-walla.

Eight years later Morris Eisenberg sailing from Lübeck
Entered the States through the still-wounded port of Galveston.

1908, eeloo hotesy, hotesy-ahnoo, hotesy ahnoo mi-Mizraim.
Or you could say "Morris" was his name. A Moshe.

Ippa Fano wanna bella woh. The New Orleans musician called
Professor Longhair was named Henry Roeland Byrd.

Not heroic not nostalgic not learnëd. Made-up names:
Hum a few bars and we'll homme-la-la. Woh ohma-dallah.

Longhair or Henry and his wife Alice joined the Civil Defense
Special Forces 714. Alice was a Colonel, he a Lieutenant.

Here they are in uniforms and caps, pistols in holsters.
Hotesy anno, Ippa Fano trah ma dollah, tra la la.

Morris took the name "Eisenberg" after the rich man from
His shtetl who in 1908 owned a town in Arkansas.

Most of this is made up, but the immigration papers did
Require him to renounce all loyalty to Czar Nicholas.

As he signed to that, he must have thought to himself
The Yiddish equivalent of *No Problem*, Mah la belle.

Hotesy hotesy-ahno. Wella-mallah widda dallah,
Mah fanna-well. A townful of people named Eisenberg.

The past is not decent or orderly, it is made-up and devious.
The man was correct when he said it's not even past.

Look up at the waters from the causeway where you stand:
Lime causeway made of grunts and halfway-forgettings

On a foundation of crushed oyster shells. Roadbed
Paved with abandonments, shored up by haunts.

Becky was a teenager married to an older man. After she
Met Morris, in 1910 or so, she swapped Eisenbergs.

They rode out of Arkansas on his motorcycle, well-ah-way.
Wed-away. "Mizraim" is Egypt, I remember that much.

The storm bulldozed Galveston with a great rake of debris,
In the September heat the smell of the dead was unbearable.

Hotesy hotesy ahnoo. "Professor" the New Orleans title
For any piano player. He had a Caribbean left hand,

A boogie-woogie right. Civil Defense Special Forces 714
Organized for disasters, mainly hurricanes. Floods.

New Orleans style borrowing this and that, ah wail-ah-way la-la,
They probably got "714" from Joe Friday's badge number

On *Dragnet*. Jack Webb chose the number in memory
Of Babe Ruth's 714 home runs, the old record.

As living memory of the great hurricanes of the thirties
And the fifties dissolved, Civil Defense Forces 714

Also dissolved, washed away for well or ill—yet nothing
Ever entirely abandoned though generations forget, and ah

Well the partial forgetting embellishes everything all the more:
Alla-mallah, mi-Mizraim, try my tra-la, hotesy-totesy.

Dollars, dolors. Callings and contrivances. King Zulu. Comus.
Sephardic ju-ju and verses. Voodoo mojo, Special Forces.

Henry formed a group named Professor Longhair and his
Shuffling Hungarians. After so much renunciation

And invention, is this the image of the promised end?
All music haunted by all the music of the dead forever.

Becky haunted forever by Pearl the daughter she abandoned
For love, O try my tra-la-la, ma la belle, mah walla-woe.

Blessed is He who came to Earth as a Bull
And ravished our virgin mother and ran with her
Astride his back across the plains and mountains
Of the whole world. And when He came to Ocean,
He swam across with our mother on his back.
And in His wake the peoples of the world
Sailed trafficking in salt, oil, slaves and opal.
Hallowed be His name, who blesses the nations:
From the Middle Kingdom, gunpowder and Confucius.
From Europe, Dante and the Middle Passage.
Shiva is His lieutenant, and by His commandment
Odysseus brought the palm tree to California,
Tea to the Britons, opium to the Cantonese.
Horses, tobacco, tomatoes and gonorrhea
Coursed by His will between Old Worlds and New.
In the Old Market where children once were sold,
Pirated music and movies in every tongue,
Defying borders as Algebra trans-migrated
From Babylon to Egypt. At His beck
Empire gathers, diffuses, and in time disperses
Into the smoky Romance of its name.
And after the great defeat in Sicily
When thousands of Athenians were butchered
Down in the terrible quarries, and many were bound

And branded on the face with a horse's head,
Meaning *this man is a slave,* a few were spared
Because they could recite new choruses
By the tragedian Euripides, whose works
And fame had reached to Sicily—as willed
By the Holy One who loves blood sacrifice
And burnt offerings, commerce and the Arts.

KEYBOARD

A disembodied piano. The headphones allow
The one who touches the keys a solitude
Inside his music; shout and he may not turn:

Image of the soul that thinks to turn from the world.
Serpent-scaled Apollo skins the naive musician
Alive: then Marsyas was sensitive enough

To feel the whole world in a touch. In Africa
The raiders with machetes to cut off hands
Might make the victim choose, "long sleeve or short."

Shahid Ali says it happened to Kashmiri weavers,
To kill the art. There are only so many stories.
The Loss. The Chosen. And even before The Journey,

The Turning: the fruit from any tree, the door
To any chamber, but this one—and the greedy soul,
Blade of the lathe. The Red Army smashed pianos,

But once they caught an SS man who could play.
They sat him at the piano and pulled their fingers
Across their throats to explain that they would kill him

When he stopped playing, and so for sixteen hours
They drank and raped while the Nazi fingered the keys.
The great Song of the World. When he collapsed

Sobbing at the instrument they stroked his head
And blew his brains out. Cold-blooded Orpheus turns
Again to his keyboard to improvise a plaint:

Her little cries of pleasure, blah-blah, the place
Behind her ear, lilacs in rain, a sus-chord,
A phrase like a moonlit moth in tentative flight,

O lost Eurydice, blah-blah. His archaic head
Kept singing after the body was torn away:
Body, old long companion, supporter—the mist

Of oranges, la-la-la, the smell of almonds,
The taste of olives, her woolen skirt. The great old
Poet said, What should we wear for the reading—necktie?

Or better no necktie, turtleneck? The head
Afloat turns toward Apollo to sing and Apollo,
The cool-eyed rainbow lizard, plies the keys.

BOOK

Its leaves flutter, they thrive or wither, its outspread
Signatures like wings open to form the gutter.

The pages riffling brush my fingertips with their edges:
Whispering, erotic touch this hand knows from ages back.

What progress we have made, they are burning my books, not
Me, as once they would have done, said Freud in 1933.

A little later, the laugh was on him, on the Jews,
On his sisters. O people of the book, wanderers, *anderes*.

When we've wandered all our ways, said Ralegh, Time shuts up
The story of our days—Ralegh beheaded, his life like a book.

The sound *bk*: lips then palate, outward plosive to interior stop.
Bk, bch: the beech tree, pale wood incised with Germanic runes.

Enchanted wood. Glyphs and characters between boards.
The reader's dread of finishing a book, that loss of a world,

And also the reader's dread of beginning a book, becoming
Hostage to a new world, to some spirit or spirits unknown.

Look! What thy mind cannot contain you can commit
To these waste blanks. The jacket ripped, the spine cracked,

Still it arouses me, torn crippled god like Loki the schemer
As the book of Lancelot aroused Paolo and Francesca

Who cling together even in Hell, O passionate, so we read.
Love that turns or torments or comforts me, love of the need

Of love, need for need, columns of characters that sting
Sometimes deeper than any music or movie or picture,

Deeper sometimes even than a body touching another.
And the passion to make a book—passion of the writer

Smelling glue and ink, sensuous. The writer's dread of making
Another tombstone, my marker orderly in its place in the stacks.

Or to infiltrate and inhabit another soul, as a splinter of spirit
Pressed between pages like a wildflower, odorless, brittle.

JAR OF PENS

Sometimes the sight of them
Huddled in their cylindrical formation
Repels me: humble, erect,
Mute and expectant in their
Rinsed-out honey crock: my quiver
Of detached stingers. (Or, a bouquet
Of lies and intentions unspent.)

Pilots, drones, workers. The Queen is
Cross. Upright lodge
Of the toilworthy, gathered
At attention as though they believe
All the ink in the world could
Cover the first syllable
Of one heart's confusion.

This fat fountain pen wishes
In its elastic heart
That I were the farm boy
Whose illiterate father
Rescued it out of the privy
After it fell from the boy's pants:
The man digging in boots
By lanternlight, down in the pit.

Another pen strains to call back
The characters of the thousand
World languages dead since 1900,
Curlicues, fiddleheads, brushstroke
Splashes and arabesques:
Footprints of extinct species.

The father hosed down his boots
And leaving them in the barn
With his pants and shirt
Came into the kitchen,
Holding the little retrieved
Symbol of symbol-making.

O brood of line-scratchers, plastic
Scabbards of the soul, you have
Outlived the sword—talons and
Wingfeathers for the hand.

OTHER HAND

The lesser twin,
The one whose accomplishments
And privileges are unshowy: getting to touch
The tattoo on my right shoulder.
Wearing the mitt.

I feel its familiar weight and textures
As the adroit one rests against it for a moment.
They twine fingers.

Lefty continues to experience considerable
Difficulty expressing himself clearly
And correctly in writing.

Comparison with his brother prevents him
From putting forth his best effort.

Yet this halt one too has felt a breast, thigh,
Clasped an ankle or most intimate
Of all, the fingers of a hand.

And possibly his trembling touch,
As less merely adept and confident,
Is subtly the more welcome of the two.

In the Elysian Fields, where every defect
Will be compensated and the last
Will be first, this one will lead skillfully
While the other will assist.

And as my shadow stalks that underworld
The right hand too will rejoice—released
From its long burden of expectation:
The yoke of dexterity finally laid to rest.

IMMATURE SONG

I have heard that adolescence is a recent invention,
A by-product of progress, one of Capitalism's

Suspended transitions between one state and another,
Like refugee camps, internment camps, like the Fields

Of Concentration in a campus catalogue. Summer
Camps for teenagers. When I was quite young

My miscomprehension was that "Concentration Camp"
Meant where the scorned were admonished to concentrate,

Humiliated: forbidden to let the mind wander away.
"Concentration" seemed just the kind of punitive euphemism

The adult world used to coerce, like the word "Citizenship"
On the report cards, graded along with disciplines like History,

English, Mathematics. Citizenship was a field or
Discipline in which for certain years I was awarded every

Marking period a "D" meaning Poor. Possibly my first political
Emotion was wishing they would call it Conduct, or Deportment.

The indefinitely suspended transition of the refugee camps
Must be a poor kind of refuge—subjected to capricious

Kindness and requirements and brutality, the unchampioned
Refugees kept between childhood and adulthood, having neither.

In the Holy Land for example, or in Mother Africa.
At that same time of my life when I heard the abbreviation

"DP" for Displaced Person I somehow mixed it up with
"DTs" for Delirium Tremens, both a kind of stumbling called

By a childish nickname. And you my poem, you are like
An adolescent: confused, awkward, self-preoccupied, vaguely

Rebellious in a way that lacks practical focus, moving without
Discipline from thing to thing. Do you disrespect Authority merely

Because it speaks so badly, because it deploys the lethal bromides
With a clumsy conviction that offends your delicate senses?—but if

Called on to argue such matters as the refugees you mumble and
Stammer, poor citizen, you get sullen, you sigh and you look away.

THE FORGETTING

The forgetting I notice most as I get older is really a form of memory:
The undergrowth of things unknown to you young, that I have forgotten.

Memory of so much crap, jumbled with so much that seems to matter.
Lieutenant Calley. Captain Easy. Mayling Soong. Sibby Sisti.

And all the forgettings that preceded my own: Baghdad, Egypt, Greece,
The Plains, centuries of lootings of antiquities. Obscure atrocities.

Imagine!—a big tent filled with mostly kids, yelling for poetry. In fact
It happened, I was there in New Jersey at the famous poetry show.

I used to wonder, what if the Baseball Hall of Fame overflowed
With too many thousands of greats all in time unremembered?

Hardly anybody can name all eight of their great-grandparents.
Can you? Will your children's grandchildren remember your name?

You'll see, you little young jerks: your favorite music and your political
Furors, too, will need to get sorted in dusty electronic corridors.

In 1972, Chou En-lai was asked the lasting effects of the French
Revolution: "Too soon to tell." Remember?—or was it Mao Tse-tung?

Poetry made of air strains to reach back to Begats and suspiring
Forward into air, grunting to beget the hungry or overfed Future.

Ezra Pound praises the Emperor who appointed a committee of scholars
To pick the best 450 Noh plays and destroy all the rest, the fascist.

The stand-up master Steven Wright says he thinks he suffers from
Both amnesia and déjà vu: "I feel like I have forgotten this before."

Who remembers the arguments when jurors gave Pound the only prize
For poetry awarded by the United States Government? Until then.

I was in the big tent when the guy read his poem about how the Jews
Were warned to get out of the Twin Towers before the planes hit.

The crowd was applauding and screaming, they were happy—it isn't
That they were anti-Semitic, or anything. They just weren't listening. Or

No, they were listening, but that certain way. In it comes, you hear it, and
That selfsame second you swallow it or expel it: an ecstasy of forgetting.

LOUIE LOUIE

I have heard of Black Irish but I never
Heard of White Catholic or White Jew.
I have heard of "Is Poetry Popular?" but I
Never heard of Lawrence Welk Drove
Sid Caesar Off Television.

I have heard of Kwanzaa but I have
Never heard of Bert Williams.
I have never heard of Will
Rogers or Roger Williams
Or Buck Rogers or Pearl Buck
Or Frank Buck or *Frank
Merriwell At Yale.*

I have heard of Yale but I never
Heard of George W. Bush.
I have heard of Harvard but I
Never heard of Numerus Clausus
Which sounds to me like
Some kind of Pig Latin.

I have heard of the Pig Boy.
I have never heard of the Beastie

Boys or the Scottsboro Boys but I
Have heard singing Boys, what
They were called I forget.

I have never heard America
Singing but I have heard of I
Hear America Singing, I think
It must have been a book
We had in school, I forget.

POEM WITH LINES IN ANY ORDER

Sonny said *Then he shouldn't have given Molly the two more babies.*

Dave's sister and her husband adopted the baby, and that was Babe.

You can't live in the past.

Sure he was a tough guy but he was no hero.

Sonny and Toots went to live for a while with the Braegers.

It was a time when it seemed like everybody had a nickname.

Nobody can live in the future.

When Rose died having Babe, Dave came after the doctor with a gun.

Toots said *What would you expect, he was a young man, there she was.*

Sonny still a kid himself when Dave moved out on Molly.

The family gave him Rose's cousin Molly as a wife, to raise the children.

There's no way to just live in the present.

In their eighties Toots and Sonny still arguing about their father.

Dave living above the bar with Della and half the family.

POEM OF

DISCONNECTED PARTS

At Robben Island the political prisoners studied.
They coined the motto *Each one Teach one.*

In Argentina the torturers demanded the prisoners
Address them always as *"Profesor."*

Many of my friends are moved by guilt, but I
Am a creature of shame, I am ashamed to say.

Culture the lock, culture the key. Imagination
That calls boiled sheep heads in the market "Smileys."

The first year at Guantánamo, Abdul Rahim Dost
Incised his Pashto poems into styrofoam cups.

"The Sangomo says in our Zulu culture we do not
Worship our ancestors: we consult them."

Becky is abandoned in 1902 and Rose dies giving
Birth in 1924 and Sylvia falls in 1951.

Still falling still dying still abandoned in 2006
Still nothing finished among the descendants.

I support the War, says the comic, it's just the Troops
I'm against: can't stand those Young People.

Proud of the fallen, proud of her son the bomber.
Ashamed of the government. Skeptical.

After the Klansman was found Not Guilty one juror
Said she just couldn't vote to convict a pastor.

Who do you write for? I write for dead people:
For Emily Dickinson, for my grandfather.

"The Ancestors say the problem with your Knees
Began in your Feet. It could move up your Back."

But later the Americans gave Dost not only paper
And pen but books. Hemingway, Dickens.

Old Aegyptius said Whoever has called this Assembly,
For whatever reason — that is a good in itself.

O thirsty shades who regard the offering, O stained earth.
There are many fake Sangomos. This one is real.

Coloured prisoners got different meals and could wear
Long pants and underwear, Blacks got only shorts.

No he says he cannot regret the three years in prison:
Otherwise he would not have written those poems.

I have a small-town mind. Like the Greeks and Trojans.
Shame. Pride. Importance of looking bad or good.

Did he see anything like the prisoner on a leash? Yes,
In Afghanistan. In Guantánamo he was isolated.

Our enemies "disassemble" says the President.
Not that anyone at all couldn't mis-speak.

The *profesores* created nicknames for torture devices:
The Airplane. The Frog. Burping the Baby.

Not that those who behead the helpless in the name
Of God or tradition don't also write poetry.

Guilts, metaphors, traditions. Hunger strikes.
Culture the penalty. Culture the escape.

What could your children boast about you? What
Will your father say, down among the shades?

The Sangomo told Marvin, "*You are crushed by some
Weight. Only your own Ancestors can help you.*"

EURYDICE AND STALIN

She crossed a bridge, and looking down she saw
The little Georgian boiling in a trench of blood.
He hailed her, and holding up his one good arm

He opened his palm to show her two pulpy seeds
Like droplets—one for each time she lost her life.
Then in a taunting voice he chanted some verses.

Poetry was popular in Hell, the shades
Recited lines they had memorized—forgetful
Even of who they were, but famished for life.

And who was she? The little scoundrel below her
Opened his palm again to show that the seeds
Had multiplied, there was one for every month

He held her child hostage, or each false poem
He extorted from her. He smiled a curse and gestured
As though to offer her a quenching berry.

On certain pages of her printed books
She had glued new handwritten poems to cover
The ones she was ashamed of: now could he want

Credit as her patron, for those thickened pages?
He said she was the canary he had blinded
To make it sing. Her courage, so much birdseed.

Shame, endless revision, inexhaustible art:
The hunchback loves his hump. She crossed the bridge
And wandered across a field of steaming ashes.

Was it a government or an impassioned mob
That tore some poet to pieces? She struggled to recall
The name, and was it herself, a radiant O.

AKHMATOVA'S

"SUMMER GARDEN"

I want to return to that unique garden walled
By the most magnificent ironwork in the world

Where the statues remember me young and I remember
Them the year they were underwater

And in fragrant silence
Under a royal colonnade of lindens

I imagine the creaking of ships' masts and the swan
Floats over the centuries admiring its flawless twin.

Asleep there like the dead are hundreds of thousands
Of footfalls of friends and enemies, enemies and friends

The procession of those shades is endless
From the granite urn to the doorway of the palace

Where my white nights of those years whisper
About some love grand and mysterious

And everything glows like mother-of-pearl and jasper
Though the source of that light also is mysterious.

THE WAVE

(Virgil, Georgics III:237–244)

As when far off in the middle of the ocean
A breast-shaped curve of wave begins to whiten
And rise above the surface, then rolling on
Gathers and gathers until it reaches land
Huge as a mountain and crashes among the rocks
With a prodigious roar, and what was deep
Comes churning up from the bottom in mighty swirls
Of sunken sand and living things and water —

So in the springtime every race of people
And all the creatures on earth or in the water,
Wild animals and flocks and all the birds
In all their painted colors,
                                        all rush to charge
Into the fire that burns them: love moves them all.

ANTIQUE

I drowned in the fire of having you, I burned
In the river of not having you, we lived
Together for hours in a house of a thousand rooms
And we were parted for a thousand years.
Ten minutes ago we raised our children, who cover
The earth and have forgotten that we existed.
It was not maya, it was not a ladder to perfection,
It was this cold sunlight falling on this warm earth.

When I turned you went to Hell. When your ship
Fled the battle I followed you and lost the world
Without regret but with stormy recriminations.
Someday far down that corridor of horror the future
Someone who buys this picture of you for the frame
At a stall in a dwindled city will study your face
And decide to harbor it for a little while longer
From the waters of anonymity, the acids of breath.

FROM THE LAST

CANTO OF PARADISE

(Paradiso XXXIII: 46–48, 52–66)

As I drew nearer to the end of all desire,
I brought my longing's ardor to a final height,
Just as I ought. My vision, becoming pure,

Entered more and more the beam of that high light
That shines on its own truth. From then, my seeing
Became too large for speech, which fails at a sight

Beyond all boundaries, at memory's undoing—
As when the dreamer sees and after the dream
The passion endures, imprinted on his being

Though he can't recall the rest. I am the same:
Inside my heart, although my vision is almost
Entirely faded, droplets of its sweetness come

The way the sun dissolves the snow's crust—
The way, in the wind that stirred the light leaves,
The oracle that the Sibyl wrote was lost.

FROM

JERSEY RAIN

2000

SAMURAI SONG

When I had no roof I made
Audacity my roof. When I had
No supper my eyes dined.

When I had no eyes I listened.
When I had no ears I thought.
When I had no thought I waited.

When I had no father I made
Care my father. When I had
No mother I embraced order.

When I had no friend I made
Quiet my friend. When I had no
Enemy I opposed my body.

When I had no temple I made
My voice my temple. I have
No priest, my tongue is my choir.

When I have no means fortune
Is my means. When I have
Nothing, death will be my fortune.

Need is my tactic, detachment
Is my strategy. When I had
No lover I courted my sleep.

VESSEL

What is this body as I fall asleep again?
What I pretended it was when I was small:

A crowded vessel, a starship or submarine
Dark in its dark element, a breathing hull,

Arms at the flanks, the engine heart and brain
Pulsing, feet pointed like a diver's, the whole

Resolutely diving through the oblivion
Of night with living cargo. O carrier shell

That keeps your trusting passengers from All:
Some twenty-thousand times now you have gone

Out into blackness tireless as a seal,
Blind always as a log, but plunging on

Across the reefs of coral that scrape the keel —
O veteran immersed from toe to crown,

Buoy the population of the soul
Toward their destination before they drown.

ODE TO MEANING

Dire one and desired one,
Savior, sentencer—

In an old allegory you would carry
A chained alphabet of tokens:

Ankh Badge Cross.
Dragon,
Engraved figure guarding a hallowed intaglio,
Jasper kinema of legendary Mind,
Naked omphalos pierced
By quills of rhyme or sense, torah-like: unborn
Vein of will, xenophile
Yearning out of Zero.

Untrusting I court you. Wavering
I seek your face, I read
That Crusoe's knife
Reeked of you, that to defile you
The soldier makes the rabbi spit on the torah.
"I'll drown my book" says Shakespeare.

Drowned walker, revenant.
After my mother fell on her head, she became

More than ever your sworn enemy. She spoke
Sometimes like a poet or critic of forty years later.
Or she spoke of the world as Thersites spoke of the heroes,
"I think they have swallowed one another. I
Would laugh at that miracle."

You also in the laughter, warrior angel:
Your helmet the zodiac, rocket-plumed
Your spear the beggar's finger pointing to the mouth
Your heel planted on the serpent Formulation
Your face a vapor, the wreath of cigarette smoke crowning
Bogart as he winces through it.

You not in the words, not even
Between the words, but a torsion,
A cleavage, a stirring.

You stirring even in the arctic ice,
Even at the dark ocean floor, even
In the cellular flesh of a stone.

Gas. Gossamer. My poker friends
Question your presence
In a poem by me, passing the magazine
One to another.

Not the stone and not the words, you
Like a veil over Arthur's headstone,
The passage from Proverbs he chose

While he was too ill to teach
And still well enough to read, *I was*
Beside the master craftsman
Delighting him day after day, ever
At play in his presence—you

A soothing veil of distraction playing over
Dying Arthur playing in the hospital,
Thumbing the Bible, fuzzy from medication,
Ever courting your presence.
And you the prognosis,
You in the cough.

Gesturer, when is your spur, your cloud?
You in the airport rituals of greeting and parting.
Indicter, who is your claimant?
Bell at the gate. Spiderweb iron bridge.
Cloak, video, aroma, rue, what is your
Elected silence, where was your seed?

What is Imagination
But your lost child born to give birth to you?

Dire one. Desired one.
Savior, sentencer—

Absence,
Or presence ever at play:
Let those scorn you who never

Starved in your dearth. If I
Dare to disparage
Your harp of shadows I taste
Wormwood and motor oil, I pour
Ashes on my head. You are the wound. You
Be the medicine.

A B C

Any body can die, evidently. Few
Go happily, irradiating joy,

Knowledge, love. Many
Need oblivion, painkillers,
Quickest respite.

Sweet time unafflicted,
Various world:

X = your zenith.

AN ALPHABET OF MY DEAD

In the dark bed, against the insomnia and its tedium, I have told them over many times: a game not morbid but reassuring. Evidence that I exist, sleepless.

■

Harry Antonucci, who used to play basketball at the Jewish Community Center, as many Italian kids did, paying five dollars to join the same way a Jewish boy might find it convenient to join the YMCA.

A year ahead of me in school, tall, a good ballplayer though one eye was milky dull, skewed away from where his good eye was looking. A sourpuss, swinging his head in an irritable way and too ready to call fouls against himself. In contrast, his graceful, soft jump shot.

The scowl and his swaying walk seemed to express anger at having a bad eye. We made fun of him for being grouchy and half blind.

But as we got older he became "popular." He died in a car full of football players, class officers, a blond girl named Cornelia Wells who was Harry's date. She was bruised and scarred; he was the only one killed.

It surprised me that a grumpy, one-eyed Italian who swayed sideways when he walked would be going out with Neil Wells. But one day trying to remember him I realized he had been handsome: fine features, white skin, dark curly hair.

And years after that I realized that a girl might be attracted by that wounded manner, by the shadow of a lost eye.

∎

B, C, D. Some poets. Elizabeth Bishop. Her last public appearance was at the Grolier Book Shop, an afternoon signing party for my second book of poetry. Then afterwards, getting ready for dinner, the sudden stroke.

A "good death," but she didn't get to witness the upsurge in her reputation. Nor Cummings the decline in his. Even before I learned about his right-wing politics, the Red-baiting and anti-Semitism, I came to dislike the person behind the poems that once attracted me. The reliance on charm came to seem grim, unrelenting.

My college friend Henry Dumas, shot dead by a cop in a subway car a few years after graduation. Smart, talented, feckless, a bit of a phony, the first person my age to have a wife and child.

I knew just enough to like him for refusing the Negro stereotypes of the time: communications-major frat boy, street tough, jock. His knit cap, his knowledge of the Bible, his fear as he once explained to me that his wife's father saw through him. His beautiful little boy.

∎

Becky Eisenberg, my mother's mother. As a teenager she married an older man, a distant cousin, also an Eisenberg. They lived in Arkansas, in a settlement of Jews who had all taken the same last name, that of the rich man from their village in Russia. In that village of Eisenbergs outside Little Rock, Becky gave birth to the older Eisenberg's daughter, Pearl. Then another cousin, Morris Eisenberg, her own age, came to town on his motorcycle—my grandfather.

When my mother was crazy, Becky, my Nana, took care of me. She was afraid of everything: cars, the mailman, electricity, dogs. Were these fears rooted in shame she felt for divorcing the first Eisenberg? Or had there been no divorce?

Morris and Becky left Arkansas together with the child Pearl. My mother, Sylvia, remembers her half-sister Pearl teaching her how to brush her teeth. One day they took Pearl to the station in Baltimore and put her on a train, and that was the last Sylvia saw or heard of her.

It must have been 1922 or 1923. Becky and Morris are dead, probably Pearl too, and for the story I depend on Sylvia, who is the spirit of confusion and darkness incarnate. Except for what she says, the story is locked away among the dead forever.

■

Souls, vaporous mirrors, registers for me of my difference from them. Robert Fitzgerald and Mason Gross, my philosophy teacher—learned gentlemen, with the gift for study, which I lack. Equally unlike me, in a different way, Lynda Hull, almost as young when she died as Henry

Dumas was. Her recklessness as alien as Fitzgerald's and Gross's scholarship, each difference producing an oddly similar note of constraint, a cordial awkwardness, when I was with her or one of them.

Drugs, drink. The wistfully lurid movies of her poetry, neon and rain and facepaint. The books and languages of Fitzgerald and Gross. Neighbors to my soul, but not like my soul.

Army Ippolito, football coach and Spanish teacher. When he didn't know what else to do in class, he had us sing, *Ya las gaviotas tien' sus alas abren, sus alas para volar. Miles de conchas tien' las arenas, y perlas tien' la mar!* Or something like that.

One day in need of a digression Army told the class how when he was young my grandfather, Dave Pinsky, took him to Yankee Stadium. Army got claustrophobia on the subway, became sweaty and panicky. My grandfather was amused and callous, he showed no mercy.

This hardness was a quality Army admired, and I took reflected glory from that, as I believe he intended, which was generous of him. This out-of-it, skinny ineffectual Jewish boy: I knew his grandfather, said Army, he was a tough guy and my benefactor.

And I did learn a little Spanish, one of the few things of the kind I have ever mastered. So in college I read Cervantes and Gongora. Armand, Hippolytus, thank you for that and for your kindness.

■

A drowsy spell: it is working. Plural dead like counting sheep, J for the exterminated Jews of Europe, K the obliviated Kallikaks of New Jersey, the dead Laborers who framed and plastered these bedroom walls threaded by other dead hands with snaking electrical wires and the dendritic systems of pipes, audible.

■

Nan M., my high school girlfriend, dead of lung cancer in her thirties. Bill Nestrick, Mrs. Olmstead. Dave Pinsky, the tough guy who took Army Ippolito to Yankee Stadium, and who died of heart failure at my present age. Last week, my Aunt Thelma told me that Sylvia, my mother, tried to keep Dave from seeing me. Why?

■

Sir Arthur Quiller-Couch, in *The Oxford Book of English Verse*, 1900, rev. 1939, omitted the stanza of George Gascoigne's "Lullaby of a Lover" in which the sixteenth-century poet refers to his penis. Yvor Winters told me about this omission with great amusement, in 1963. All dead, Quiller-Couch, Winters, Gascoigne, who in his poem does something like what I am doing now:

Sing lullaby, as women do,
     Wherewith they bring their babes to rest:
And lullaby can I sing too,
     As womanly as can the best.
With lullaby, they still the child;
And if I be not much beguiled,

Full many wanton babes have I,
Which must be still'd with lullaby.

Quiller-Couch prints the stanzas in which Gascoigne puts to sleep his eyes, his youth, his will, but omits the next-to-last:

Eke lullaby my loving boy,
    My little Robin, take thy rest;
Since age is cold and nothing coy,
    Keep close thy coin, for so is best;
With lullaby be thou content,
With lullaby thy lusts relent,
Let others pay which hath mo pence;
Thou art too poor for such expense.

It pleased me to have Winters share this joke on the prudery of Sir Arthur Quiller-Couch. Now, Quiller-Couch has something like a last laugh on us as the opprobrious term "phallocentric" rises on the great wheel turned by the engine of death, always churning, as Gascoigne reminds himself:

Thus lullaby, my youth, mine eyes,
    My will, my ware, and all that was.
I can no mo delays devise,
    But welcome pain, let pleasure pass;
With lullaby now take your leave,
With lullaby your dreams deceive;
And when you rise with waking eye,
Remember then this lullaby.

■

Self-destroyers. Carl R., in the eighth grade, the big inoffensive pudgy blond boy who drowned. Jed S., the MIT student who took my poetry class at Wellesley and presented his poems on long scrolls of computer paper, the all-capitals dot matrix lines nearly unreadable. The first computer printouts I'd ever seen.

They found Jed in his room with a plastic bag over his head, possibly to enhance a drug or masturbation. In the MIT literary magazine he published a dialogue between "Socrates" and "S." At the end, Socrates says, "S., your arguments have refuted me completely—there is nothing more I can say."

T., the graduate student who was caught stealing.

■

U the completely unknown, all the millions like dry leaves whose lives, rounded or cut off, touched mine not at all.

■

Butch Voorhees, the middle son of a family that lived in the rooming house next door. That miserable neighborhood was stratified: my building housed only families, both buildings allowed only white people. Butch and two brothers and his drunken father and the mother lived in one large room over the *porte-cochère* of a house full of hard-drinking housepainters, laborers, restaurant workers.

He died in the Navy, some kind of accident. When the father, all but a derelict by then, recognized me in a bar years later, he asked me to buy him a drink. Maudlin, sentimental, dirty. Huck Finn's father.

"*Porte-cochère*" was my mother's word. Once she saw me helping Butch carry home a can of kerosene for their heating stove. He lugged it for ten steps, then I did my ten steps, taking turns all the way from Burroughs' Hardware.

Sylvia scolded me for this. She said the kerosene was to kill the lice on their heads: "Stay away from them, or you'll be covered with *vermin*."

I had seen the stove in that room carpeted everywhere with bedding and clothes, a double hot plate and tiny sink in one corner: the kerosene was for the stove. I couldn't see that it wasn't the vermin she feared, precisely, but some worse contagion of poverty or doom.

■

Old Mr. and Mrs. Williams who lived in a velvet shingle house behind those houses on Rockwell Avenue. I thought they had no electricity because the iceman delivered ice for their icebox. With tongs and a rubber pad on his shoulder. Their house, a phantom from another century.

■

X the unknown ancestors of my eight great-grandparents, unseen multitudes who have created my body, thousands of them reaching back into time, tens of thousands, kings and slaves, savages and sages, warriors and rapists, victims and perpetrators.

And also the unknown ancestors of this language I write in, the creators of the music I hear and the machines I use, this machine I type at—all the dead fanning back from the apex of this moment to the unthinkably wide fishtail wake of causes.

■

Not YAHWEH but Yetta of *Yetta's Market* on Rockwell Avenue, at the railroad crossing, the little frame storefront tacked onto the frame house. Jerry Lewis invented a song, "Yetta, I'll Never Forget Huh."

■

Zagreus, ancient god of the past, dead one, give me my honey measure of sleep.

THE GREEN PIANO

Aeolian. Gratis. Great thunderer, half-ton infant of miracles
Torn free of charge from the universe by my mother's will.
You must have amazed that half-respectable street

Of triple-decker families and rooming-house housepainters
The day that the bole-ankled oversized hams of your legs
Bobbed in procession up the crazy-paved front walk

Embraced by the arms of Mr. Poppik the seltzer man
And Corydon his black-skinned helper, tendering your thighs
Thick as a man up our steps. We are not reptiles:

Even the male body bears nipples, as if to remind us
We are designed for dependence and nutriment, past
Into future. O Europe, they budged your case, its ponderous

Guts of iron and brass, ten kinds of hardwood and felt
Up those heel-pocked risers and treads splintering tinder.
Angelic nurse of clamor, yearner, tinkler, dominator—

O Elephant, you were for me! When the tuner Mr. Otto Van Brunt
Pronounced you excellent despite the cracked sounding board, we
Obeyed him and swabbed your ivories with hydrogen peroxide.

You blocked a doorway and filled most of the living room.
The sofa and chairs dwindled to a ram and ewes, cowering: now,
The colored neighbors could be positive we were crazy and rich,

As we thought the people were who gave you away for the moving
Out of their carriage house — they had painted you the color of pea soup.
The drunk man my mother hired never finished antiquing you

Ivory and umber, so you stood half done, a throbbing mistreated noble,
Genuine — my mother's swollen livestock of love: lost one, unmastered:
You were the beast she led to the shrine of my genius, mistaken.

Endlessly I bonged according to my own chord system *Humoresque,*
The Talk of the Town, What'd I Say. Then one day they painted you pink.
Pink is how my sister remembers you the Saturday afternoon

When our mother fell on her head, dusty pink as I turn on the bench
In my sister's memory to see them carrying our mother up the last
Steps and into the living room, inaugurating the reign of our confusion.

They sued the builder of the house she fell in, with the settlement
They bought a house at last and one day when I came home from college
You were gone, mahogany breast, who nursed me through those

Years of the Concussion, and there was a crappy little Baldwin Acrosonic
In your place, gleaming, walnut shell. You were gone, despoiled one —
Pink one, forever-green one, white-and-gold one, comforter, a living soul.

TO TELEVISION

Not a "window on the world"
But as we call you,
A box a tube

Terrarium of dreams and wonders.
Coffer of shades, ordained
Cotillion of phosphors
Or liquid crystal

Homey miracle, tub
Of acquiescence, vein of defiance.
Your patron in the pantheon would be Hermes

Raster dance,
Quick one, little thief, escort
Of the dying and comfort of the sick,

In a blue glow my father and little sister sat
Snuggled in one chair watching you
Their wife and mother was sick in the head
I scorned you and them as I scorned so much

Now I like you best in a hotel room,
Maybe minutes

Before I have to face an audience: behind
The doors of the armoire, box
Within a box—Tom & Jerry, or also brilliant
And reassuring, Oprah Winfrey.

Thank you, for I watched, I watched
Sid Caesar speaking French and Japanese not
Through knowledge but imagination,
His quickness, and Thank you, I watched live
Jackie Robinson stealing

Home, the image—O strung shell—enduring
Fleeter than light like these words we
Remember in: they too are winged
At the helmet and ankles.

BIOGRAPHY

Stone wheel that sharpens the blade that mows the grain.
Wheel of the sunflower turning, wheel that turns
The spiral press that squeezes the oil expressed
From grain or olives. Particles turned to mud
On the potter's wheel that whirls to form the vessel
That holds the oil that drips to cool the blade.

My mother's dreadful fall. Her mother's dread
Of all things: death, life, birth. My brother's birth
Just before the fall. His birth again in Jesus.
Wobble and blur of my soul, born just once,
That cleaves to circles. The moon, the eye, the year,
Circle of causes or chaos or turns of chance.

Line of a tune as it cycles back to the root,
Arc of the changes. The line from there to here
Of Ellen speaking, thread of my circle of friends.
The art of lines, a chord of the circle of work.
Radius. Lives of children growing away.
The plant radiant in air, its root in dark.

THE HAUNTED RUIN

Even your computer is a haunted ruin, as your
Blood leaves something of itself, warming
The tool in your hand.

From far off, down the billion corridors
Of the semiconductor, military
Pipes grieve at the junctures.

This too smells of the body, its hot
Polymers smell of breast milk
And worry-sweat.

Hum of so many cycles in voltage,
Carbon-fed. Sing, wires. Feel, hand. Eyes,
Watch and form

Legs and bellies of characters:
Beak and eye of A. Serpentine hiss
S of the foregoers, claw-tines

Of E and of the claw hammer
You bought yesterday, its head
Tasting of light oil, the juice

Of dead striving—the haft
Of ash, for all its urethane varnish,
Polished by body salts.

Pull, clawhead. Hold, shaft. Steel face,
Strike and relieve me. Maker's
Voice audible in the baritone

Whine of the handsaw working.
Last harbor of long-dead names of
Adana or Vilna. Machine-soul.

JERSEY RAIN

Now near the end of the middle stretch of road
What have I learned? Some earthly wiles. An art.
That often I cannot tell good fortune from bad,
That once had seemed so easy to tell apart.

The source of art and woe aslant in wind
Dissolves or nourishes everything it touches.
What roadbank gullies and ruts it doesn't mend
It carves the deeper, boiling tawny in ditches.

It spends itself regardless into the ocean.
It stains and scours and makes things dark or bright:
Sweat of the moon, a shroud of benediction,
The chilly liquefaction of day to night,

The Jersey rain, my rain, soaks all as one:
It smites Metuchen, Rahway, Saddle River,
Fair Haven, Newark, Little Silver, Bayonne.
I feel it churning even in fair weather

To craze distinction, dry the same as wet.
In ripples of heat the August drought still feeds
Vapors in the sky that swell to drench my state —
The Jersey rain, my rain, in streams and beads

Of indissoluble grudge and aspiration:
Original milk, replenisher of grief,
Descending destroyer, arrowed source of passion,
Silver and black, executioner, font of life.

FROM NEW POEMS IN

THE FIGURED WHEEL

1996

GINZA SAMBA

A monosyllabic European called Sax
Invents a horn, walla whirledy wah, a kind of twisted
Brazen clarinet, but with its column of vibrating
Air shaped not in a cylinder but in a cone
Widening ever outward and bawaah spouting
Infinitely upward through an upturned
Swollen golden bell rimmed
Like a gloxinia flowering
In Sax's Belgian imagination

And in the unfathomable matrix
Of mothers and fathers as a genius graven
Humming into the cells of the body
Or saved cupped in the resonating grail
Of memory changed and exchanged
As in the trading of brasses,
Pearls and ivory, calicos and slaves,
Laborers and girls, two

Cousins in a royal family
Of Niger known as the Birds or Hawks.
In Christendom one cousin's child
Becomes a "favorite negro" ennobled
By decree of the Czar and founds
A great family, a line of generals,

Dandies and courtiers including the poet
Pushkin, killed in a duel concerning
His wife's honor, while the other cousin sails

In the belly of a slaveship to the port
Of Baltimore where she is raped
And dies in childbirth, but the infant
Will marry a Seminole and in the next
Chorus of time their child fathers
A great Hawk or Bird, with many followers
Among them this great-grandchild of the Jewish
Manager of a Pushkin estate, blowing

His American breath out into the wiggly
Tune uncurling its triplets and sixteenths—the Ginza
Samba of breath and brass, the reed
Vibrating as a valve, the aether, the unimaginable
Wires and circuits of an ingenious box
Here in my room in this house built
A hundred years ago while I was elsewhere:

It is like falling in love, the atavistic
Imperative of some one
Voice or face—the skill, the copper filament,
The golden bellful of notes twirling through
Their invisible element from
Rio to Tokyo and back again gathering
Speed in the variations as they tunnel
The twin haunted labyrinths of stirrup
And anvil echoing here in the hearkening
Instrument of my skull.

POEM WITH REFRAINS

The opening scene. The yellow, coal-fed fog
Uncurling over the tainted city river,
A young girl rowing and her anxious father
Scavenging for corpses. Funeral meats. The clever
Abandoned orphan. The great athletic killer
Sulking in his tent. As though all stories began
With someone dying.

               When her mother died,
My mother refused to attend the funeral—
In fact, she sulked in her tent all through the year
Of the old lady's dying, I don't know why:
She said, because she loved her mother so much
She couldn't bear to see the way the doctors,
Or her father, or—someone—was letting her mother die.
"Follow your saint, follow with accents sweet;
Haste you, sad notes, fall at her flying feet."

She fogs things up, she scavenges the taint.
Possibly that's the reason I write these poems.

But they did speak: on the phone. Wept and argued,
So fiercely one or the other often cut off
A sentence by hanging up in rage—like lovers,
But all that year she never saw her face.

They lived on the same block, four doors apart.
"Absence my presence is; strangeness my grace;
With them that walk against me is my sun."

"Synagogue" is a word I never heard,
We called it *shul*, the Yiddish word for school.
Elms, terra-cotta, the ocean a few blocks east.
"Lay institution": she taught me we didn't think
God lived in it. The rabbi just a teacher.

But what about the hereditary priests,
Descendants of the Cohanes of the Temple,
Like Walter Holtz — I called him Uncle Walter,
When I was small. A big man with a face
Just like a boxer dog or a cartoon sergeant.
She told me whenever he helped a pretty woman
Try on a shoe in his store, he'd touch her calf
And ask her, "How does that feel?" I was too little
To get the point but pretended to understand.
"Desire, be steady; hope is your delight,
An orb wherein no creature can be sorry."

She didn't go to my bar mitzvah, either.
I can't say why: she was there, and then she wasn't.
I looked around before I mounted the steps
To chant that babble and the speech the rabbi wrote
And there she wasn't, and there was Uncle Walter
The Cohane frowning with his doggy face:
"She's missing her own son's *musaf*." Maybe she just
Doesn't like rituals. Afterwards, she had a reason

I don't remember. I wasn't upset: the truth
Is, I had decided to be the clever orphan
Some time before. By now, it's all a myth.
What is a myth but something that seems to happen
Always for the first time over and over again?
And ten years later, she missed my brother's, too.
I'm sorry: I think it was something about a hat.
"Hot sun, cool fire, tempered with sweet air,
Black shade, fair nurse, shadow my white hair;
Shine, sun; burn, fire; breathe, air, and ease me."

She sees the minister of the Nation of Islam
On television, though she's half-blind in one eye.
His bow tie is lime, his jacket crocodile green.
Vigorously he denounces the Jews who traded in slaves,
The Jews who run the newspapers and the banks.
"I see what this guy is mad about now," she says,
"It must have been some Jew that sold him the suit."
"And the same wind sang and the same wave whitened,
And or ever the garden's last petals were shed,
In the lips that had whispered, the eyes that had lightened."

But when they unveiled her mother's memorial stone,
Gathered at the graveside one year after the death,
According to custom, while we were standing around
About to begin the prayers, her car appeared.
It was a black car; the ground was deep in snow.
My mother got out and walked toward us, across
The field of gravestones capped with snow, her coat
Black as the car, and they waited to start the prayers

Until she arrived. I think she enjoyed the drama.
I can't remember if she prayed or not,
But that may be the way I'll remember her best:
Dark figure, awaited, attended, aware, apart.
"The present time upon time passëd striketh;
With Phoebus's wandering course the earth is graced.

The air still moves, and by its moving, cleareth;
The fire up ascends, and planets feedeth;
The water passeth on, and all lets weareth;
The earth stands still, yet change of changes breedeth."

HOUSE HOUR

Now the pale honey of a kitchen light
Burns at an upstairs window, the sash a cross.
Milky daylight moon,
Sky scored by phone lines. Houses in rows
Patient as cows.

Dormers and gables of an immigrant street
In a small city, the wind-worn afternoon
Shading into night.

Hundreds of times before
I have felt it in some district
Of shingle and downspout at just this hour.
The renter walking home from the bus
Carrying a crisp bag. Maybe a store
Visible at the corner, neon at dusk.
Macaroni mist on the glass.

Unwilled, seductive as music, brief
As dusk itself, the forgotten mirror
Brushed for dozens of years
By the same gray light, the same shadows
Of soffit and beam end, a reef
Of old snow glowing along the walk.

If I am hollow, or if I am heavy with longing, the same:
The ponderous houses of siding,
Fir framing, horsehair plaster, fired bricks
In a certain light, changing nothing, but touching
Those separate hours of the past
And now at this one time
Of day touching this one, last spokes
Of light silvering the attic dust.

STREET MUSIC

Sweet Babylon, headphones. Song bones.
At a slate stairway's base, alone and unready,
Not far from the taxis and bars
Around the old stone station,
In the bronze, ordinary afternoon light—
To find yourself back behind that real
City and inside this other city
Where you slept in the street.
Your bare feet, gray tunic of a child,
Coarse sugar of memory.

Salt Nineveh of barrows and stalls,
The barber with his copper bowl,
Beggars and grain-sellers,
The alley of writers of letters
In different dialects, stands
Of the ear-cleaner, tailor,
Spicer. Reign of Asur-Banipal.
Hemp woman, whore merchant,
Hand porter, errand boy,
Child sold from a doorway.

Candy Memphis of exile and hungers.
Honey kalends and drays,

Syrup-sellers and sicknesses,
Runes, donkeys, yams, tunes
On the mouth-harp, shuffles
And rags. Healer, dealer, drunkard.
Fresh water, sewage—wherever
You died in the market sometimes
Your soul flows a-hunting buried
Cakes here in the city.

SOOT

Archaic, the trains mated with our human blood.
Stone trestle, abutment wall. Above the tracks
A rakish exile Santa lashed to a pole.
Black cinders, burdock, sumac, Pepsi, cellophane,
Each syllable a filament in the cord
Of a word-net knotted in the passionate shadows
Of skeletal vine and beanpole in one back yard
Along the embankment. Here with dirty thunder
Deliberate, heavy creatures before the light
Of morning made the bedroom windows tremble
With lordly music, and their exhalations
Tingled our nostrils. Railbed tavern and church
Of former slaves, synagogue of the low,
Sicilian grocery, Polish crèche. A seed
Of particles that Zeuslike penetrated
The bread and carboned the garden tomatoes—even
Our sheets that bucked and capered in the wind
Flashed whiter than others, tempered by iron black
Bleaching to armor in silver winter sun.

THE DAY DREAMERS

All day all over the city every person
Wanders a different city, sealed intact
And haunted as the abandoned subway stations
Under the city. Where is my alley doorway?

Stone gable, brick escarpment, cliffs of crystal.
Where is my terraced street above the harbor,
Café and hidden workshop, house of love?
Webbed vault, tiled blackness. Where is my park, the path

Through conifers, my iron bench, a shiver
Of ivy and margin birch above the traffic?
A voice. *There is a mountain and a wood
Between us* — one wrote, lovesick — *Where the late*

Hunter and the bird have seen us. Aimless at dusk,
Heart muttering like any derelict,
Or working all morning, violent with will,
Where is my garland of lights? My silver rail?

THE CITY DARK

In the early winter dusk the broken city dark
Seeps from the tunnels. Up towers and in gusty alleys,

The mathematical veil of generation has lit its torches
To light the rooms of the mated and unmated: the two

Fated behind you and four behind them in the matrix
Widening into the past, eight, sixteen, thirty-two,

Many as the crystal dream cells illuminating the city.
Even for those who sleep in the street there are lights.

Like a heavy winter sleep the long flint cold of the past
Spreads over the glinting dream-blisters of the city, asleep

Or awake, as if the streets were an image of the channels
Of time, with sixty-four, one hundred and twenty-eight,

The ancestral net of thousands only a couple of centuries back,
With its migrations and fortunes and hungers like an image

Of the city where the star-dispelling lights have climbed
And multiplied over the tenements and outlying suburbs

Like a far past of multitudes behind us in the glistering web
Of strands crossing, thousands and tens of thousands

Of lives coupled with their gains, passions, misfortunes.
Somewhere in the tangled alleyways, a rape. Somewhere

A spirit diffused winglike, blind along the stretched wires
Branching the dark city air or bundled under the streets,

Coursing surely to some one face like an ancient song Do re,
Re la sol sol. Somewhere misfortune, somewhere recognition.

Back here one died of starvation, here one thrived. Descendant,
The bitter city work and the shimmering maternal burden

Of music uncoil outward on the avenues through smoky bars,
By televisions, beyond sleepers while the oblivion of generation

Radiates backward and then forward homeward to the one voice
Or face like an underground pool, through its delicate lightshaft

Moonlit, a cistern of light, echoing in a chamber cellared under
The dark of the city pavement, the faintly glittering slabs.

THE ICE-STORM

In Memory of Bernie Fields

Dear Robert, Thank you for trying to rig
A conduit for me — linkage, blank, bandage, this
Contraption made of grammar, with "I" for "he":

■

Words are no clumsier than what we use to trace
Tangled-up branches on the family tree
Of some culprit virus stowed in the rootclot.

■

Voice not you nor I, I not what I was or am,
You not what you are or were — poker crony,
Acquaintance, seeking what germ strewn in the sodcloud?

■

Flailing for an instructive failure: *"That's life,"*
Muttered — not an adage and not an answer
To *What is life?* (Not my field, but nearly.)

■

What is a life?: that is the far profounder question,
As I'd have said even before the cancer
Churned me across dark water to this other side:

■

No opalescent study house, no sidelocked sages.
No smoking field where a hero craves a cottage.
No void no terraces no planisphere. Nothing you know.

■

The day that Leslie read those poems to me
He wasn't sure I was listening, dark shape
Unspeaking on the pillows. Tell him I was.

■

What is a life? A specimen, or a kind?
A savage craving or civil obituary
Architecture of birth, attachment, achievement?—

■

The *Times* rehearsing with mediated, Roman
Sweetness the names of my near kin, so cherished
In the molten hold of attachment, sweet cooling lava;

■

Or honey of ink aggrandizing, gratifying
("... one of the great virologists of the century"),
Meaning: a success, like everybody else.

■

When you hear the *Yisgadal v'yiskadash sh'may rabaw*
When the beloved one hurling her handful of earth
Staggers at the brink as if buffeted by wind

■

When the congregation responds *Y'hay sh-may*
Rabaw m'varah, l'aulom ul-al-maya—it's
Now my mouth is the flared bell of a silver horn

■

Now my eyes lidded by the wings of a dragonfly look
Inward for billions of miles, Now my feet are two
Crystals that leave no footprints. O the poker game!

■

Closed system, boyish ritual first Sunday evening
Of the month, more innocent than boyish, none smoking, few
Cursing, never more than a second beer, game, lightness

■

Wanting deeply to win, and that wanting what we play
To laugh at, stakes high enough to terrify our
Selves at fourteen, low enough to parody that fear.

■

My brain a clay vessel my fingers unlit candles
My lights a cello, cabalistic rhythms of Spade
Heart Club Diamonds royalty in Gypsy embroidery.

■

Permission, remission, the Washington AIDS job
My doctors said was too great a risk for me. Now
My heart is fluted amber, umbrage of texts, When

■

Thou cut down thy harvest in the field, and hast forgot
A sheaf in the field, thou shalt not go again to
Fetch it, for it will be for the stranger,

■

The fatherless and the widow, remember thou
Lived a bondsman in the land of Egypt. *Yisgadal
V'yiskadash* trembling life, crystal or viral,

■

Lifespan of the ice-storm the week after I died
That lasted for three days: separate lucid twigs
Still coated with chrism each morning, gutters

■

Still filigreed with leaf-ice, diamonded branches
Bowed heavy with light, at dusk still rosy,
Mysterious light melted to a sheen by morning.

INCANTATION

From the Polish of Czeslaw Milosz

Human reason is beautiful and invincible.
No bars, no barbed wire, no pulping of books,
No sentence of banishment can prevail against it.
It establishes the universal ideas in language,
And guides our hand so we write Truth and Justice
With capital letters, lie and oppression with small.
It puts what should be above things as they are,
It is an enemy of despair and a friend of hope.
It does not know Jew from Greek or slave from master,
Giving us the estate of the world to manage.
It saves austere and transparent phrases
From the filthy discord of tortured words.
It says that everything is new under the sun,
Opens the congealed fist of the past.
Beautiful and very young are Philo-Sophia
And poetry, her ally in the service of the good.
As late as yesterday Nature celebrated their birth,
The news was brought to the mountains by a unicorn and an echo,
Their friendship will be glorious, their time has no limit,
Their enemies have delivered themselves to destruction.

SONG ON PORCELAIN

From the Polish of Czeslaw Milosz

Rose-colored cup and saucer,
Flowery demitasses:
They lie beside the river
Where an armored column passes.
Winds from across the meadow
Sprinkle the banks with down;
A torn apple tree's shadow
Falls on the muddy path;
The ground everywhere is strewn
With bits of brittle froth—
Of all things broken and lost
The porcelain troubles me most.

Before the first red tones
Begin to warm the sky
The earth wakes up, and moans.
It is the small sad cry
Of cups and saucers cracking,
The masters' precious dream
Of roses, of mowers raking
And shepherds on the lawn.
The black underground stream

Swallows the frozen swan.
This morning, as I walked past
The porcelain troubled me most.

The blackened plain spreads out
To where the horizon blurs
In a litter of handle and spout,
A lively pulp that stirs
And crunches under my feet.
Pretty, useless foam:
Your stained colors are sweet—
Some bloodstained, in dirty waves
Flecking the fresh black loam
In the mounds of these new graves.
In sorrow and pain and cost
The porcelain troubles me most.

IF YOU COULD WRITE ONE
GREAT POEM, WHAT WOULD
YOU WANT IT TO BE ABOUT?

*(Asked of four student poets at the
Illinois School for the Visually Impaired)*

Fire: because it is quick, and can destroy.
Music: place where anger has its place.
Romantic Love—the cold or stupid ask why.
Sign: that it is a language, full of grace,

That it is visible, invisible, dark and clear,
That it is loud and noiseless and is contained
Inside a body and explodes in air
Out of a body to conquer from the mind.

IMPOSSIBLE TO TELL

To Robert Hass and in memory of Elliot Gilbert

Slow dulcimer, gavotte and bow, in autumn,
Bashō and his friends go out to view the moon;
In summer, gasoline rainbow in the gutter,

The secret courtesy that courses like ichor
Through the old form of the rude, full-scale joke,
Impossible to tell in writing. "Bashō"

He named himself, "Banana Tree": banana
After the plant some grateful students gave him,
Maybe in appreciation of his guidance

Threading a long night through the rules and channels
Of their collaborative linking-poem
Scored in their teacher's heart: live, rigid, fluid

Like passages etched in a microscopic circuit.
Elliot had in his memory so many jokes
They seemed to breed like microbes in a culture

Inside his brain, one so much making another
It was impossible to tell them all:
In the court-culture of jokes, a top banana.

Imagine a court of one: the queen a young mother,
Unhappy, alone all day with her firstborn child
And her new baby in a squalid apartment

Of too few rooms, a different race from her neighbors.
She tells the child she's going to kill herself.
She broods, she rages. Hoping to distract her,

The child cuts capers, he sings, he does imitations
Of different people in the building, he jokes,
He feels if he keeps her alive until the father

Gets home from work, they'll be okay till morning.
It's laughter versus the bedroom and the pills.
What is he in his efforts but a courtier?

Impossible to tell his whole delusion.
In the first months when I had moved back East
From California and had to leave a message

On Bob's machine, I used to make a habit
Of telling the tape a joke; and part-way through,
I would pretend that I forgot the punchline,

Or make believe that I was interrupted—
As though he'd be so eager to hear the end
He'd have to call me back. The joke was Elliot's,

More often than not. The doctors made the blunder
That killed him some time later that same year.
One day when I got home I found a message

On my machine from Bob. He had a story
About two rabbis, one of them tall, one short,
One day while walking along the street together

They see the corpse of a Chinese man before them,
And Bob said, sorry, he forgot the rest.
Of course he thought that his joke was a dummy,

Impossible to tell—a dead-end challenge.
But here it is, as Elliot told it to me:
The dead man's widow came to the rabbis weeping,

Begging them, if they could, to resurrect him.
Shocked, the tall rabbi said absolutely not.
But the short rabbi told her to bring the body

Into the study house, and ordered the shutters
Closed so the room was night-dark. Then he prayed
Over the body, chanting a secret blessing

Out of Kabala. "Arise and breathe," he shouted;
But nothing happened. The body lay still. So then
The little rabbi called for hundreds of candles

And danced around the body, chanting and praying
In Hebrew, then Yiddish, then Aramaic. He prayed
In Turkish and Egyptian and Old Galician

For nearly three hours, leaping about the coffin
In the candlelight so that his tiny black shoes
Seemed not to touch the floor. With one last prayer

Sobbed in the Spanish of before the Inquisition
He stopped, exhausted, and looked in the dead man's face.
Panting, he raised both arms in a mystic gesture

And said, "Arise and breathe!" And still the body
Lay as before. Impossible to tell
In words how Elliot's eyebrows flailed and snorted

Like shaggy mammoths as—the Chinese widow
Granting permission—the little rabbi sang
The blessing for performing a circumcision

And removed the dead man's foreskin, chanting blessings
In Finnish and Swahili, and bathed the corpse
From head to foot, and with a final prayer

In Babylonian, gasping with exhaustion,
He seized the dead man's head and kissed the lips
And dropped it again and leaping back commanded,

"Arise and breathe!" The corpse lay still as ever.
At this, as when Bashō's disciples wind
Along the curving spine that links the *renga*

Across the different voices, each one adding
A transformation according to the rules
Of stasis and repetition, all in order

And yet impossible to tell beforehand,
Elliot changes for the punchline: the wee
Rabbi, still panting, like a startled boxer,

Looks at the dead one, then up at all those watching,
A kind of Mel Brooks gesture: "Hoo boy!" he says,
"Now that's what I call *really dead*." O mortal

Powers and princes of earth, and you immortal
Lords of the underground and afterlife,
Jehovah, Raa, Bol-Morah, Hecate, Pluto,

What has a brilliant, living soul to do with
Your harps and fires and boats, your bric-a-brac
And troughs of smoking blood? Provincial stinkers,

Our languages don't touch you, you're like that mother
Whose small child entertained her to beg her life.
Possibly he grew up to be the tall rabbi,

The one who washed his hands of all those capers
Right at the outset. Or maybe he became
The author of these lines, a one-man *renga*

The one for whom it seems to be impossible
To tell a story straight. It was a routine
Procedure. When it was finished the physicians

Told Sandra and the kids it had succeeded,
But Elliot wouldn't wake up for maybe an hour,
They should go eat. The two of them loved to bicker

In a way that on his side went back to Yiddish,
On Sandra's to some Sicilian dialect.
He used to scold her endlessly for smoking.

When she got back from dinner with their children
The doctors had to tell them about the mistake.
Oh swirling petals, falling leaves! The movement

Of linking *renga* coursing from moment to moment
Is meaning, Bob says in his Haiku book.
Oh swirling petals, all living things are contingent,

Falling leaves, and transient, and they suffer.
But the Universal is the goal of jokes,
Especially certain ethnic jokes, which taper

Down through the swirling funnel of tongues and gestures
Toward their preposterous Ithaca. There's one
A journalist told me. He heard it while a hero

Of the South African freedom movement was speaking
To elderly Jews. The speaker's own right arm
Had been blown off by right-wing car-bombers.

He told his listeners they had to cast their ballots
For the ANC—a group the old Jews feared
As "in with the Arabs." But they started weeping

As the old one-armed fighter told them their country
Needed them to vote for what was right, their vote
Could make a country their children could return to

From London and Chicago. The moved old people
Applauded wildly, and the speaker's friend
Whispered to the journalist, "It's the Belgian Army

Joke come to life." I wish I could tell it
To Elliot. In the Belgian Army, the feud
Between the Flemings and Walloons grew vicious,

So out of hand the army could barely function.
Finally one commander assembled his men
In one great room, to deal with things directly.

They stood before him at attention. "All Flemings,"
He ordered, "to the left wall." Half the men
Clustered to the left. "Now all Walloons," he ordered,

"Move to the right." An equal number crowded
Against the right wall. Only one man remained
At attention in the middle: "What are you, soldier?"

Saluting, the man said, "Sir, I am a Belgian."
"Why, that's astonishing, Corporal—what's your name?"
Saluting again, "Rabinowitz," he answered:

A joke that seems at first to be a story
About the Jews. But as the *renga* describes
Religious meaning by moving in drifting petals

And brittle leaves that touch and die and suffer
The changing winds that riffle the gutter swirl,
So in the joke, just under the raucous music

Of Fleming, Jew, Walloon, a courtly allegiance
Moves to the dulcimer, gavotte and bow,
Over the banana tree the moon in autumn—

Allegiance to a state impossible to tell.

FROM

THE
WANT
BONE

1990

THE WANT BONE

The tongue of the waves tolled in the earth's bell.
Blue rippled and soaked in the fire of blue.
The dried mouthbones of a shark in the hot swale
Gaped on nothing but sand on either side.

The bone tasted of nothing and smelled of nothing,
A scalded toothless harp, uncrushed, unstrung.
The joined arcs made the shape of birth and craving
And the welded-open shape kept mouthing O.

Ossified cords held the corners together
In groined spirals pleated like a summer dress.
But where was the limber grin, the gash of pleasure?
Infinitesimal mouths bore it away,

The beach scrubbed and etched and pickled it clean.
But O I love you it sings, my little my country
My food my parent my child I want you my own
My flower my fin my life my lightness my O.

SHIRT

The back, the yoke, the yardage. Lapped seams,
The nearly invisible stitches along the collar
Turned in a sweatshop by Koreans or Malaysians

Gossiping over tea and noodles on their break
Or talking money or politics while one fitted
This armpiece with its overseam to the band

Of cuff I button at my wrist. The presser, the cutter,
The wringer, the mangle. The needle, the union,
The treadle, the bobbin. The code. The infamous blaze

At the Triangle Factory in nineteen-eleven.
One hundred and forty-six died in the flames
On the ninth floor, no hydrants, no fire escapes —

The witness in a building across the street
Who watched how a young man helped a girl to step
Up to the windowsill, then held her out

Away from the masonry wall and let her drop.
And then another. As if he were helping them up
To enter a streetcar, and not eternity.

A third before he dropped her put her arms
Around his neck and kissed him. Then he held
Her into space, and dropped her. Almost at once

He stepped to the sill himself, his jacket flared
And fluttered up from his shirt as he came down,
Air filling up the legs of his gray trousers—

Like Hart Crane's Bedlamite, "shrill shirt ballooning."
Wonderful how the pattern matches perfectly
Across the placket and over the twin bar-tacked

Corners of both pockets, like a strict rhyme
Or a major chord. Prints, plaids, checks,
Houndstooth, Tattersall, Madras. The clan tartans

Invented by millowners inspired by the hoax of Ossian,
To control their savage Scottish workers, tamed
By a fabricated heraldry: MacGregor,

Bailey, MacMartin. The kilt, devised for workers
To wear among the dusty clattering looms.
Weavers, carders, spinners. The loader,

The docker, the navvy. The planter, the picker, the sorter
Sweating at her machine in a litter of cotton
As slaves in calico headrags sweated in fields:

George Herbert, your descendant is a Black
Lady in South Carolina, her name is Irma
And she inspected my shirt. Its color and fit

And feel and its clean smell have satisfied
Both her and me. We have culled its cost and quality
Down to the buttons of simulated bone,

The buttonholes, the sizing, the facing, the characters
Printed in black on neckband and tail. The shape,
The label, the labor, the color, the shade. The shirt.

FROM THE CHILDHOOD OF JESUS

One Saturday morning he went to the river to play.
He modeled twelve sparrows out of the river clay

And scooped a clear pond, with a dam of twigs and mud.
Around the pond he set the birds he had made,

Evenly as the hours. Jesus was five. He smiled,
As a child would who had made a little world

Of clear still water and clay beside a river.
But a certain Jew came by, a friend of his father,

And he scolded the child and ran at once to Joseph,
Saying, "Come see how your child has profaned the Sabbath,

Making images at the river on the Day of Rest."
So Joseph came to the place and took his wrist

And told him, "Child, you have offended the Word."
Then Jesus freed the hand that Joseph held

And clapped his hands and shouted to the birds
To go away. They raised their beaks at his words

And breathed and stirred their feathers and flew away.
The people were frightened. Meanwhile, another boy,

The son of Annas the scribe, had idly taken
A branch of driftwood and leaning against it had broken

The dam and muddied the little pond and scattered
The twigs and stones. Then Jesus was angry and shouted,

"Unrighteous, impious, ignorant, what did the water
Do to harm you? Now you are going to wither

The way a tree does, you shall bear no fruit
And no leaves, you shall wither down to the root."

At once, the boy was all withered. His parents moaned,
The Jews gasped, Jesus began to leave, then turned

And prophesied, his child's face wet with tears:
"Twelve times twelve times twelve thousands of years

Before these heavens and this earth were made,
The Creator set a jewel in the throne of God

With Hell on the left and Heaven to the right,
The Sanctuary in front, and behind, an endless night

Endlessly fleeing a Torah written in flame.
And on that jewel in the throne, God wrote my name."

Then Jesus left and went into Joseph's house.
The family of the withered one also left the place,

Carrying him home. The Sabbath was nearly over.
By dusk, the Jews were all gone from the river.

Small creatures came from the undergrowth to drink
And foraged in the shadows along the bank.

Alone in his cot in Joseph's house, the Son
Of Man was crying himself to sleep. The moon

Rose higher, the Jews put out their lights and slept,
And all was calm and as it had been, except

In the agitated household of the scribe Annas,
And high in the dark, where unknown even to Jesus

The twelve new sparrows flew aimlessly through the night,
Not blinking or resting, as if never to alight.

LAMENT FOR THE MAKERS

What if I told you the truth? What if I could?
The nuptial trek of the bower apes in May:
At night in the mountain meadow their clucking cries,

The reeking sulphur springs called Smoking Water,
Their skimpy ramparts of branches, pebbles and vines—
So slightly better than life, that snarl of weeds,

The small-town bank by comparison is Rome,
With its four-faced bronze clock that chimes the hours,
The six great pillars surmounted by a frieze

Of Chronos eating his children—or trying to,
But one child bests him because we crave to live,
And if that too means dying then to die

Like Arthur when ladies take him in his barge
Across the misty water: better than life,
Or better than truly dying. In the movies

Smoking and driving are better, a city walk.
Grit on the sidewalk after a thaw, mild air.
I took the steps along the old stone trestle

Above the station, to the part of town
I never knew, old houses flush to the street
Curving uphill. Patches of ice in the shade.

What if I found an enormous secret there
And told you? We would still feel something next
Or even at the same time. Just as now. In Brooklyn,

Among the diamond cutters at their benches
Under high Palladian windows full of a storm,
One wearing headphones listens to the Talmud.

What if he happens to feel some saw or maxim
Inwardly? Then the young girl in her helmet,
An allegorical figure called The Present,

Would mime for us the action of coming to life:
A crease of shadow across her face, a cross,
And through the window, washing stumps of brick,

Exuberant streaks and flashes—literal lightning
Spilling out into a cheery violent rain.
Worship is tautological, with its Blessed

Art thou O Lord who consecrates the Sabbath
Unto us that we may praise it in thy name
Who blesses us with this thy holy day

That we may hallow it unto thy holy blessings . . .
And then the sudden curt command or truth:
God told him, Thou shalt cut thy foreskin off.

Then Abraham was better than life. The monster
Is better when he startles us. Hurt is vivid,
Sincerity visible in the self-inflicted wound.

Paws bleeding from their terrible climb, they weave
Garlands of mountain creeper for their bed.
The circle of desire, that aches to play

Or sings to hear the song passing. We sense
How much we might yet make things change, renewed
As when the lovers rise from their bed of play

And dress for supper and from a lewd embrace
Undress again. Weeds mottle the fissured pavement
Of the playground in a net of tufted lines

As sunset drenches a cinematic honey
Over the stucco terraces, copper and blue,
And the lone player cocks wrist and ball behind

His ear and studies the rusty rim again.
The half-ruined city around him throbs and glows
With pangs of allure that flash like the names of bars

Along San Pablo Avenue: Tee Tee's Lounge,
The Mallard Club, Quick's Little Alaska, Ruthie's,
Chiquita's, and inside the sweet still air

Of tobacco, malt and lime, and in some music
But in others only voices or even quiet,
And the player's arm pauses and pumps again.

WINDOW

Our building floated heavily through the cold
On shifts of steam the raging coal-fed furnace
Forced from the boiler's hull. In showers of spark
The trolleys flashed careening under our cornice.
My mother Mary Beamish who came from Cork
Held me to see the snowfall out the window—
Windhold she sometimes said, as if in Irish
It held wind out, or showed us that wind was old.
Wind-hole in Anglo-Saxon: faces like brick,
They worshipped Eastre's rabbit, and mistletoe
That was Thor's jissom where thunder struck the oak.
We took their language in our mouth and chewed
(Some of the consonants drove us nearly crazy
Because we were Chinese—or was that just the food
My father brought from our restaurant downstairs?)
In the fells, by the falls, the Old Ghetto or New Jersey,
Little Havana or Little Russia—I forget,
Because the baby wasn't me, the way
These words are not. Whoever she was teaching to talk,
Snow she said, *Snow*, and you opened your small brown fist
And closed it and opened again to hold the reflection
Of torches and faces inside the window glass
And through it, a cold black sheen of shapes and fires

Shaking, kitchen lights, flakes that crissed and crossed
Other lights in lush diagonals, the snowcharmed traffic
Surging and pausing—red, green, white, the motion
Of motes and torches that at her word you reached
Out for, where you were, it was you, that bright confusion.

THE HEARTS

The legendary muscle that wants and grieves,
The organ of attachment, the pump of thrills
And troubles, clinging in stubborn colonies

Like pulpy shore-life battened on a jetty.
Slashed by the little deaths of sleep and pleasure,
They swell in the nurturing spasms of the waves,

Sucking to cling; and even in death itself—
Baked, frozen—they shrink to grip the granite harder.
"Rid yourself of attachments and aversions"—

But in her father's orchard, already, he says
He'd like to be her bird, and she says: Sweet, yes,
Yet I should kill thee with much cherishing,

Showing that she knows already—as Art Pepper,
That first time he takes heroin, already knows
That he will go to prison, and knows he'll suffer

And says he needs to have it, or die; and the one
Who makes the General lose the world for love
Lets him say, *would I had never seen her*, but Oh!

Says Enobarbus, Then you would have missed
A wonderful piece of work, which left unseen
Would bring less glory to your travels. Among

The creatures in the rock-torn surf, a wave
Of agitation, a gasp. A scholar quips,
Shakespeare was almost certainly homosexual,

Bisexual, or heterosexual, the sonnets
Provide no evidence on the matter. He writes
Romeo an extravagant speech on tears,

In the Italian manner, his teardrops cover
His chamber window, says the boy, he calls them crystals,
Inanely, and sings them to Juliet with his heart:

The almost certainly invented heart
Which Buddha denounces, in its endless changes
Forever jumping and moving, like an ape.

Over the poor ape's head the crystal fountain
Crashes illusions, the cold salt spume of pain
And meaningless distinction, as Buddha says,

But here in the crystal shower mouths are open
To sing, it is Lee Andrews and The Hearts
In 1957, singing *I sit in my room*

Looking out at the rain, My teardrops are
Like crystals, they cover my windowpane, the turns
Of these illusions we make become their glory:

To Buddha every distinct thing is illusion
And becoming is destruction, but still we sing
In the shower. I do. In the beginning God drenched

The Emptiness with images: the potter
Crosslegged at his wheel in Benares market
Making mud cups, another cup each second

Tapering up between his fingers, one more
To sell the tea-seller at a penny a dozen,
And tea a penny a cup. The customers smash

The empties, and waves of traffic grind the shards
To mud for new cups, in turn; and I keep one here
Next to me: holding it awhile from out of the cloud

Of dust that rises from the shattered pieces,
The risen dust alive with fire, then settled
And soaked and whirling again on the wheel that turns

And looks on the world as on another cloud,
On everything the heart can grasp and throw away
As a passing cloud, with even Enlightenment

Itself another image, another cloud
To break and churn a salt foam over the heart
Like an anemone that sucks at clouds and makes

Itself with clouds and sings in clouds and covers
Its windowpane with clouds that blur and melt,
Until one clings and holds—as once in the Temple

In the time before the Temple was destroyed
A young priest saw the seraphim of the Lord:
Each had six wings, with two they covered their faces,

With two they covered their legs and feet, with two
They darted and hovered like dragonflies or perched
Like griffins in the shadows near the ceiling—

These are the visions, too barbarous for heaven
And too preposterous for belief on earth,
God sends to taunt his prophet with the truth

No one can see, that leads to who knows where.
A seraph took a live coal from the altar
And seared the prophet's lips, and so he spoke.

As the record ends, a coda in retard:
The Hearts in a shifting velvety *ah*, and *ah*
Prolonged again, and again as Lee Andrews

Reaches *ah* high for *I have to gain Faith, Hope
And Charity, God only knows the girl
Who will love me*—Oh! *if we only could

Start over again!* Then The Hearts chant the chords
Again a final time, *ah* and the record turns
Through all the music, and on into silence again.

ICICLES

A brilliant beard of ice
Hangs from the edge of the roof
As harsh and heavy as glass.
The spikes a child breaks off

Taste of wool and the sun.
In the house, some straw for a bed,
Circled by a little train,
Is the tiny image of God.

The sky is a fiery blue,
And a fiery morning light
Burns on the fresh deep snow:
Not one track in the street.

Just as the carols tell
Everything is calm and bright:
The town lying still
Frozen silver and white.

Is only one child awake,
Breaking the crystal chimes? —
Knocking them down with a stick,
Leaving the broken stems.

THE NIGHT GAME

Some of us believe
We would have conceived romantic
Love out of our own passions
With no precedents,
Without songs and poetry—
Or have invented poetry and music
As a comb of cells for the honey.

Shaped by ignorance,
A succession of new worlds,
Congruities improvised by
Immigrants or children.

I once thought most people were Italian,
Jewish or Colored.
To be white and called
Something like *Ed Ford*
Seemed aristocratic,
A rare distinction.

Possibly I believed only gentiles
And blondes could be left-handed.

Already famous
After one year in the majors,

Whitey Ford was drafted by the Army
To play ball in the flannels
Of the Signal Corps, stationed
In Long Branch, New Jersey.

A night game, the silver potion
Of the lights, his pink skin
Shining like a burn.

Never a player
I liked or hated: a Yankee,
A mere success.

But white the chalked-off lines
In the grass, white and green
The immaculate uniform,
And white the unpigmented
Halo of his hair
When he shifted his cap:

So ordinary and distinct,
So close up, that I felt
As if I could have made him up,
Imagined him as I imagined

The ball, a scintilla
High in the black backdrop
Of the sky. Tight red stitches.
Rawlings. The bleached
Horsehide white: the color
Of nothing. Color of the past

And of the future, of the movie screen
At rest and of blank paper.

"I could have." The mind. The black
Backdrop, the white
Fly picked out by the towering
Lights. A few years later
On a blanket in the grass
By the same river
A girl and I came into
Being together
To the faint muttering
Of unthinkable
Troubadours and radios.

The emerald
Theater, the night.
Another time,
I devised a left-hander
Even more gifted
Than Whitey Ford: a Dodger.
People were amazed by him.
Once, when he was young,
He refused to pitch on Yom Kippur.

AN OLD MAN

After Cavafy

Back in a corner, alone in the clatter and babble
An old man sits with his head bent over a table
And his newspaper in front of him, in the café.

Sour with old age, he ponders a dreary truth —
How little he enjoyed the years when he had youth,
Good looks and strength and clever things to say.

He knows he's quite old now: he feels it, he sees it,
And yet the time when he was young seems — was it?
Yesterday. How quickly, how quickly it slipped away.

Now he sees how Discretion has betrayed him,
And how stupidly he let the liar persuade him
With phrases: *Tomorrow. There's plenty of time. Some day.*

He recalls the pull of impulses he suppressed,
The joy he sacrificed. Every chance he lost
Ridicules his brainless prudence a different way.

But all these thoughts and memories have made
The old man dizzy. He falls asleep, his head
Resting on the table in the noisy café.

SONNET

Afternoon sun on her back,
calm irregular slap
of water against a dock.

Thin pines clamber
over the hill's top—
nothing to remember,

only the same lake
making the same
sounds under her cheek

and flashing the same color.
No one to say her name,
no need, no one to praise her,

only the lake's voice—over
and over, to keep it before her.

THE REFINERY

… our language, forged in the dark by centuries of violent pressure, underground, out of the stuff of dead life.

Thirsty and languorous after their long sleep
The old gods crooned and shuffled and shook their heads.
Dry, dry. By railroad they set out across
The desert of stars to drink the world
Our mouths had soaked in sentences: a pollen-tinted
Slurry of passion and lapsed intention. The imagined
Taste made the savage deities hiss and snort.

Their long train clicked and sighed through
Gulfs of night between the planets, then down
Through the evening fog of redwood canyons.
Fiery warehouse windows along a wharf.
Then dusk, a gash of neon: *Bar*. Black pinewoods,
Sluggish surf among the rocks, a moan
Of dreamy forgotten divinity fading
Against the walls of a town. Inside the train
A flash of dragonfly wings, an antlered brow,
Avid reptile stenches of immortal bodies.

Black night again, and then
After the bridge, a palace on the water:

The great Refinery—a million bulbs tracing
Its turreted boulevards. The castle of a person
Pronounced alive, the Corporation: a fictional
Lord real in law.

Barbicans and torches along the siding
At the central tanks, a ward of steel
Palisades, valved and chandeliered.

The muttering gods
Greedily penetrate those bright pavilions—
Libation of Benzine, Naphthalene, Asphalt,
Gasoline, Tar: syllables
Fractioned and cracked from unarticulated

Crude, the smeared keep of life that fed
On itself in pitchy darkness when the gods
Were new—inedible, volatile
And sublimated afresh to sting
Our tongues who use it, refined from oil of stone.

The gods batten on the vats, and drink up
Lovecries and memorized Chaucer, lines from movies
And songs hoarded in mortmain: exiles' charms,
Distillates of breath steeped,
Brewed and spent—as though
We were their aphids, or their bees,
That monstered up sweetness
For them while they dozed.

THE UNCREATION

The crowd at the ballpark sing, the cantor sings
Kol Nidre, and the equipment in our cars
Fills them with singing voices while we drive.

When the warlord hears his enemy is dead,
He sings his praises. The old men sang a song
And we protesters sang a song against them,

Like teams of children in a singing game;
And at the great convention all they did
They punctuated with a song: our breath

Which is an element and so a quarter
Of all creation, heated and thrown out
With all the body's force to shake our ears.

Everything said has its little secret song,
Strained higher and lower as talking we sing all day,
The sentences turned and tinted by the body:

A tune of certain pitch for questions, a tune
For *that was not a question*, a tune for *was it*,
The little tunes of begging, of coolness, of scolding.

The Mudheads dance in their adobe masks
From house to house, and sing at each the misdeeds
Of the small children inside. And we must take you,

They sing, Now we must take you, Now we must take
You back to the house of Mud. But then the parents
With presents for the Mudheads in their arms

Come singing each child's name, and buy him back:
Forgive him, give him back, we'll give you presents.
And the prancing Mudheads take the bribes, and sing.

I make a feeble song up while I work,
And sometimes even machines may chant or jingle
Some lyrical accident that takes its place

In the great excess of song that coats the world.
But after the flood the bland Immortals will come
As holy tourists to our sunken world,

To slide like sunbeams down shimmering layers of blue:
Artemis, Gog, Priapus, Jehovah and Baal,
With faces calmer than when we gave them names,

Walking our underwater streets where bones
And houses bloom fantastic spurts of coral,
Until they find our books. The pages softened

To a dense immobile pulp between the covers
Will rise at their touch in swelling plumes like smoke,
With a faint black gas of ink among the swirls,

And the golden beings shaping their mouths like bells
Will impel their breath against the weight of ocean
To sing us into the cold regard of water.

A girl sang dancing once, and shook her hair.
A young man fasting to have a powerful dream
Sang as he cut his body, to please a spirit.

But the Gods will sing entirely, the towering spumes
Dissolving around their faces will be the incense
Of their old anonymity restored

In a choral blast audible in the clouds,
An immense vibration that presses the very fish,
So through her mighty grin the whale will sing

To keep from bursting, and the tingling krill
Will sing in her jaws, the whole cold salty world
Humming oblation to what our mouths once made.

AT PLEASURE BAY

In the willows along the river at Pleasure Bay
A catbird singing, never the same phrase twice.
Here under the pines a little off the road
In 1927 the Chief of Police
And Mrs. W. killed themselves together,
Sitting in a roadster. Ancient unshaken pilings
And underwater chunks of still-mortared brick
In shapes like bits of puzzle strew the bottom
Where the landing was for Price's Hotel and Theater.
And here's where boats blew two blasts for the keeper
To shunt the iron swing-bridge. He leaned on the gears
Like a skipper in the hut that housed the works
And the bridge moaned and turned on its middle pier
To let them through. In the middle of the summer
Two or three cars might wait for the iron trusswork
Winching aside, with maybe a child to notice
A name on the stern in black-and-gold on white,
Sandpiper, Patsy Ann, Do Not Disturb,
The Idler. If a boat was running whiskey,
The bridge clanged shut behind it as it passed
And opened up again for the Coast Guard cutter
Slowly as a sundial, and always jammed halfway.
The roadbed whole, but opened like a switch,
The river pulling and coursing between the piers.

Never the same phrase twice, the catbird filling
The humid August evening near the inlet
With borrowed music that he melds and changes.
Dragonflies and sandflies, frogs in the rushes, two bodies
Not moving in the open car among the pines,
A sliver of story. The tenor at Price's Hotel,
In clown costume, unfurls the sorrow gathered
In ruffles at his throat and cuffs, high quavers
That hold like splashes of light on the dark water,
The aria's closing phrases, changed and fading.
And after a gap of quiet, cheers and applause
Audible in the houses across the river,
Some in the audience weeping as if they had melted
Inside the music. Never the same. In Berlin
The daughter of an English lord, in love
With Adolf Hitler, whom she has met. She is taking
Possession of the apartment of a couple,
Elderly well-off Jews. They survive the war
To settle here in the Bay, the old lady
Teaches piano, but the whole world swivels
And gapes at their feet as the girl and a high-up Nazi
Examine the furniture, the glass, the pictures,
The elegant story that was theirs and now
Is a part of hers. A few months later the English
Enter the war and she shoots herself in a park,
An addled, upper-class girl, her life that passes
Into the lives of others or into a place.
The taking of lives—the Chief and Mrs. W.
Took theirs to stay together, as local ghosts.
Last flurries of kisses, the revolver's barrel,

Shivers of a story that a child might hear
And half remember, voices in the rushes,
A singing in the willows. From across the river,
Faint quavers of music, the same phrase twice and again,
Ranging and building. Over the high new bridge
The flashing of traffic homeward from the racetrack,
With one boat chugging under the arches, outward
Unnoticed through Pleasure Bay to the open sea.
Here's where the people stood to watch the theater
Burn on the water. All that night the fireboats
Kept playing their spouts of water into the blaze.
In the morning, smoking pilasters and beams.
Black smell of char for weeks, the ruin already
Soaking back into the river. After you die
You hover near the ceiling above your body
And watch the mourners awhile. A few days more
You float above the heads of the ones you knew
And watch them through a twilight. As it grows darker
You wander off and find your way to the river
And wade across. On the other side, night air,
Willows, the smell of the river, and a mass
Of sleeping bodies all along the bank,
A kind of singing from among the rushes
Calling you further forward in the dark.
You lie down and embrace one body, the limbs
Heavy with sleep reach eagerly up around you
And you make love until your soul brims up
And burns free out of you and shifts and spills
Down over into that other body, and you
Forget the life you had and begin again

On the same crossing—maybe as a child who passes
Through the same place. But never the same way twice.
Here in the daylight, the catbird in the willows,
The new café, with a terrace and a landing,
Frogs in the cattails where the swing-bridge was—
Here's where you might have slipped across the water
When you were only a presence, at Pleasure Bay.

FROM

HISTORY OF MY HEART

1984

THE FIGURED WHEEL

The figured wheel rolls through shopping malls and prisons,
Over farms, small and immense, and the rotten little downtowns.
Covered with symbols, it mills everything alive and grinds
The remains of the dead in the cemeteries, in unmarked graves and oceans.

Sluiced by salt water and fresh, by pure and contaminated rivers,
By snow and sand, it separates and recombines all droplets and grains,
Even the infinite sub-atomic particles crushed under the illustrated,
Varying treads of its wide circumferential track.

Spraying flecks of tar and molten rock it rumbles
Through the Antarctic station of American sailors and technicians,
And shakes the floors and windows of whorehouses for diggers and smelters
From Bethany, Pennsylvania to a practically nameless, semi-penal New Town

In the mineral-rich tundra of the Soviet northernmost settlements.
Artists illuminate it with pictures and incised mottoes
Taken from the Ten Thousand Stories and the Register of True Dramas.
They hang it with colored ribbons and with bells of many pitches.

With paints and chisels and moving lights they record
On its rotating surface the elegant and terrifying doings
Of the inhabitants of the Hundred Pantheons of major Gods
Disposed in iconographic stations at hub, spoke and concentric bands,

And also the grotesque demi-Gods, Hopi gargoyles and Ibo dryads.
They cover it with wind-chimes and electronic instruments
That vibrate as it rolls to make an all-but-unthinkable music,
So that the wheel hums and rings as it turns through the births of stars

And through the dead-world of bomb, fireblast and fallout
Where a few doomed races of insects fumble in the smoking grasses.
It is Jesus oblivious to hurt turning to give words to the unrighteous,
And also Gogol's feeding pig that without knowing it eats a baby chick

And goes on feeding. It is the empty armor of My Cid, clattering
Into the arrows of the credulous unbelievers, a metal suit
Like the lost astronaut revolving with his useless umbilicus
Through the cold streams, neither energy nor matter, that agitate

The cold, cyclical dark, turning and returning.
Even in the scorched and frozen world of the dead after the holocaust
The wheel as it turns goes on accreting ornaments.
Scientists and artists festoon it from the grave with brilliant

Toys and messages, jokes and zodiacs, tragedies conceived
From among the dreams of the unemployed and the pampered,
The listless and the tortured. It is hung with devices
By dead masters who have survived by reducing themselves magically

To tiny organisms, to wisps of matter, crumbs of soil,
Bits of skin, microscopic flakes, which is why they are called "great,"
In their humility that goes on celebrating the turning
Of the wheel as it rolls unrelentingly over

A cow plodding through car-traffic on a street in Iaşi,
And over the haunts of Robert Pinsky's mother and father
And wife and children and his sweet self
Which he hereby unwillingly and inexpertly gives up, because it is

There, figured and pre-figured in the nothing-transfiguring wheel.

THE CHANGES

Even at sea the bodies of the unborn and the dead
Interpenetrate at peculiar angles. In a displaced channel

The crew of a tanker float by high over the heads
Of a village of makers of flint knives, and a woman

In one round hut on a terrace dreams of her grandsons
Floating through the blue sky on a bubble of black oil

Calling her in the unknown rhythms of diesel engines to come
Lie down and couple. On the ship, three different sailors

Have a brief reverie of dark, furry shanks, and one resolves
To build when he gets home a kind of round shrine or gazebo

In the small terraced garden of his house in a suburb.
In the garden, bees fumble at hydrangeas blue as crockery

While four children giggle playing School in the round gazebo.
(To one side, the invisible shaved heads of six priests

Bob above the garden's earth as they smear ash on their chests,
Trying to dance away a great epidemic; afterwards one priest,

The youngest, founds a new discipline based on the ideals
Of childlike humility and light-heartedness and learning.)

One of the sailor's children on his lunch hour years later
Writes on a napkin a poem about blue hydrangeas, bees

And a crockery pitcher. And though he is killed in a war
And the poem is burned up unread on a mass pyre with his body,

The separate molecules of the poem spread evenly over the globe
In a starlike precise pattern, as if a geometer had mapped it.

Overhead, passengers in planes cross and recross in the invisible
Ordained lanes of air traffic — some of us in the traverse

Passing through our own slightly changed former and future bodies,
Seated gliding along the black lines printed on colored maps

In the little pouches at every seat, the webs of routes bunched
To the shapes of beaks or arrowheads at the black dots of the cities.

HISTORY OF MY HEART

I

One Christmastime Fats Waller in a fur coat
Rolled beaming from a taxicab with two pretty girls
Each at an arm as he led them in a thick downy snowfall

Across Thirty-fourth Street into the busy crowd
Shopping at Macy's: perfume, holly, snowflake displays.
Chimes rang for change. In Toys, where my mother worked

Over her school vacation, the crowd swelled and stood
Filling the aisles, whispered at the fringes, listening
To the sounds of the large, gorgeously dressed man,

His smile bemused and exalted, lips boom-booming a bold
Bass line as he improvised on an expensive, tinkly
Piano the size of a lady's jewel box or a wedding cake.

She put into my heart this scene from the romance of Joy,
Coauthored by her and the movies, like her others —
My father making the winning basket at the buzzer

And punching the enraged gambler who came onto the court—
The brilliant black and white of the movies, texture
Of wet snowy fur, the taxi's windshield, piano keys,

Reflections that slid over the thick brass baton
That worked the elevator. Happiness needs a setting:
Shepherds and shepherdesses in the grass, kids in a store,

The back room of Carly's parents' shop, record-player
And paper streamers twisted in two colors: what I felt
Dancing close one afternoon with a thin blond girl

Was my amazing good luck, the pleased erection
Stretching and stretching at the idea *She likes me*,
She likes it, the thought of legs under a woolen skirt,

To see eyes "melting" so I could think *This is it*,
They're melting! Mutual arousal of suddenly feeling
Desired: *This is it: "desire"!* When we came out

Into the street we saw it had begun, the firm flakes
Sticking, coating the tops of cars, melting on the wet
Black street that reflected storelights, soft

Separate crystals clinging intact on the nap of collar
And cuff, swarms of them stalling in the wind to plunge
Sideways and cluster in spangles on our hair and lashes,

Melting to a fresh glaze on the bloodwarm porcelain
Of our faces, Hey nonny-nonny boom-boom, the cold graceful
Manna, heartfelt, falling and gathering copious

As the air itself in the small-town main street
As it fell over my mother's imaginary and remembered
Macy's in New York years before I was even born,

11

And the little white piano, tinkling away like crazy—
My unconceived heart in a way waiting somewhere like
Wherever it goes in sleep. Later, my eyes opened

And I woke up glad to feel the sunlight warm
High up in the window, a brighter blue striping
Blue folds of curtain, and glad to hear the house

Was still sleeping. I didn't call, but climbed up
To balance my chest on the top rail, cheek
Pressed close where I had grooved the rail's varnish

With sets of double tooth-lines. Clinging
With both arms, I grunted, pulled one leg over
And stretched it as my weight started to slip down

With some panic till my toes found the bottom rail,
Then let my weight slide more till I was over—
Thrilled, half-scared, still hanging high up

With both hands from the spindles. Then lower
Slipping down until I could fall to the floor
With a thud but not hurt, and out, free in the house.

Then softly down the hall to the other bedroom
To push against the door; and when it came open
More light came in, opening out like a fan

So they woke up and laughed, as she lifted me
Up in between them under the dark red blanket,
We all three laughing there because I climbed out myself.

Earlier still, she held me curled in close
With everyone around saying my name, and hovering,
After my grandpa's cigarette burned me on the neck

As he held me up for the camera, and the pain buzzed
Scaring me because it twisted right inside me;
So when she took me and held me and I curled up, sucking,

It was as if she had put me back together again
So sweetly I was glad the hurt had torn me.
She wanted to have made the whole world up,

So that it could be hers to give. So she opened
A letter I wrote my sister, who was having trouble
Getting on with her, and read some things about herself

That made her go to the telephone and call me up:
"You shouldn't open other people's letters," I said
And she said "Yes—*who taught you that?*"

—As if she owned the copyright on good and bad,
Or having followed pain inside she owned her children
From the inside out, or made us when she named us,

III

Made me Robert. She took me with her to a print-shop
Where the man struck a slug: a five-inch strip of lead
With the twelve letters of my name, reversed,

Raised along one edge, that for her sake he made
For me, so I could take it home with me to keep
And hold the letters up close to a mirror

Or press their shapes into clay, or inked from a pad
Onto all kinds of paper surfaces, onto walls and shirts,
Lengthwise on a Band-Aid, or even on my own skin—

The little characters fading from my arm, the gift
Always ready to be used again. Gifts from the heart:
Her giving me her breast milk or my name, Waller

Showing off in a store, for free, giving them
A thrill as someone might give someone an erection,
For the thrill of it—or you come back salty from a swim:

Eighteen shucked fresh oysters and the cold bottle
Sweating in its ribbon, surprise, happy birthday!
So what if the giver also takes, is after something?

So what if with guile she strove to color
Everything she gave with herself, the lady's favor
A scarf or bit of sleeve of her favorite color

Fluttering on the horseman's bloodflecked armor
Just over the heart—how presume to forgive the breast
Or sudden jazz for becoming what we want? I want

Presents I can't picture until they come,
The generator flashlight Italo gave me one Christmas:
One squeeze and the gears visibly churning in the amber

Pistol-shaped handle hummed for half a minute
In my palm, the spare bulb in its chamber under my thumb,
Secret; or, the knife and basswood Ellen gave me to whittle.

And until the gift of desire, the heart is a titular,
Insane king who stares emptily at his counselors
For weeks, drools or babbles a little, as word spreads

In the taverns that he is dead, or an impostor. One day
A light concentrates in his eyes, he scowls, alert, and points
Without a word to one pass in the cold, grape-colored peaks—

Generals and courtiers groan, falling to work
With a frantic movement of farriers, cooks, builders,
The city thrown willing or unwilling like seed

(While the brain at the same time may be settling
Into the morning *Chronicle*, humming to itself,
Like a fat person eating M&Ms in the bathtub)

Toward war, new forms of worship or migration.
I went out from my mother's kitchen, across the yard
Of the little two-family house, and into the Woods:

Guns, chevrons, swordplay, a scarf of sooty smoke
Rolled upwards from a little cratewood fire
Under the low tent of a Winesap fallen

With fingers rooting in the dirt, the old orchard
Smothered among the brush of wild cherry, sumac,
Sassafras and the stifling shade of oak

In the strip of overgrown terrain running
East from the train tracks to the ocean, woods
Of demarcation, where boys went like newly-converted

Christian kings with angels on helmet and breastplate,
Bent on blood or poaching. *There are a mountain and a woods
Between us* — a male covenant, longbows, headlocks. A pack

Of four stayed half-aware it was past dark
In a crude hut roasting meat stolen from the A&P
Until someone's annoyed father hailed us from the tracks

And scared us home to catch hell: We were worried,
Where have you been? In the Woods. With snakes and tramps.
An actual hobo knocked at our back door

One morning, declining food, to get hot water.
He shaved on our steps from an enamel basin with brush
And cut-throat razor, the gray hair on his chest

Armorial in the sunlight—then back to the woods,
And the otherlife of snakes, poison oak, boxcars.
Were the trees cleared first for the trains or the orchard?

Walking home by the street because it was dark,
That night, the smoke-smell in my clothes was like a bearskin.
Where the lone hunter and late bird have seen us

Pass and repass, the mountain and the woods seem
To stand darker than before—words of sexual nostalgia
In a song or poem seemed cloaked laments

For the woods when Indians made lodges from the skin
Of birch or deer. When the mysterious lighted room
Of a bus glided past in the mist, the faces

Passing me in the yellow light inside
Were a half-heard story or a song. And my heart
Moved, restless and empty as a scrap of something

Blowing in wide spirals on the wind carrying
The sound of breakers clearly to me through the pass
Between the blocks of houses. The horn of Roland

V

But what was it I was too young for? On moonless
Nights, water and sand are one shade of black,
And the creamy foam rising with moaning noises

Charges like a spectral army in a poem toward the bluffs
Before it subsides dreamily to gather again.
I thought of going down there to watch it awhile,

Feeling as though it could turn me into fog,
Or that the wind would start to speak a language
And change me—as if I knocked where I saw a light

Burning in some certain misted window I passed,
A house or store or tap-room where the strangers inside
Would recognize me, locus of a new life like a woods

Or orchard that waxed and vanished into cloud
Like the moon, under a spell. Shrill flutes,
Oboes and cymbals of doom. My poor mother fell,

And after the accident loud noises and bright lights
Hurt her. And heights. She went down stairs backwards,
Sometimes with one arm on my small brother's shoulder.

Over the years, she got better. But I was lost in music;
The cold brazen bow of the saxophone, its weight
At thumb, neck and lip, came to a bloodwarm life

Like Italo's flashlight in the hand. In a white
Jacket and pants with a satin stripe I aspired
To the roughneck elegance of my Grandfather Dave.

Sometimes, playing in a bar or at a high school dance,
I felt my heart following after a capacious form,
Sexual and abstract, in the thunk, thrum,

Thrum, come-wallow and then a little screen
Of quicker notes goosing to a fifth higher, winging
To clang-whomp of a major seventh: listen to *me*

Listen to *me*, the heart says in reprise until sometimes
In the course of giving itself it flows out of itself
All the way across the air, in a music piercing

As the kids at the beach calling from the water
Look, Look at me, to their mothers, but out of itself, into
The listener the way feeling pretty or full of erotic reverie

Makes the one who feels seem beautiful to the beholder
Witnessing the idea of the giving of desire—nothing more wanted
Than the little singing notes of wanting—the heart

Yearning further into giving itself into the air, breath
Strained into song emptying the golden bell it comes from,
The pure source poured altogether out and away.

THE SAVING

Though the sky still was partly light
Over the campsite clearing
Where some men and boys sat eating
Gathered near their fire,
It was full dark in the trees,
With somewhere a night-hunter
Up and out already to pad
Unhurried after a spoor,
Pausing maybe to sniff
At the strange, lifeless aura
Of a dropped knife or a coin
Buried in the spongy duff.

Willful, hungry and impatient,
Nose damp in the sudden chill,
One of the smaller, scrawnier boys
Roasting a chunk of meat
Pulled it half-raw from the coals,
Bolted it whole from the skewer,
And started to choke and strangle—
Gaping his helpless mouth,
Struggling to retch or to swallow
As he gestured, blacking out,
And felt his father lift him

And turning him upside down
Shake him and shake him by the heels,
Like a woman shaking a jar—
And the black world upside down,
The upside-down fire and sky,
Vomited back his life,
And the wet little plug of flesh
Lay under him in the ashes.
Set back on his feet again
In the ring of faces and voices,
He drank the dark air in,
Snuffling and feeling foolish

In the fresh luxury of breath
And the brusque, flattering comfort
Of the communal laughter. Later,
Falling asleep under the stars,
He watched a gray wreath of smoke
Unfurling into the blackness:
And he thought of it as the shape
Of a newborn ghost, the benign
Ghost of his death, that had nearly
Happened: it coiled, as the wind rustled,
And he thought of it as a power,
His luck or his secret name.

THE QUESTIONS

What about the people who came to my father's office
For hearing aids and glasses — chatting with him sometimes

A few extra minutes while I swept up in the back,
Addressed packages, cleaned the machines; if he was busy

I might sell them batteries, or tend to their questions:
The tall overloud old man with a tilted, ironic smirk

To cover the gaps in his hearing; a woman who hummed one
Prolonged note constantly, we called her "the hummer" — how

Could her white fat husband (he looked like Rev. Peale)
Bear hearing it day and night? And others: a coquettish old lady

In a bandeau, a European. She worked for refugees who ran
Gift shops or booths on the boardwalk in the summer;

She must have lived in winter on Social Security. One man
Always greeted my father in Masonic gestures and codes.

Why do I want them to be treated tenderly by the world, now
Long after they must have slipped from it one way or another,

While I was dawdling through school at that moment — or driving,
Reading, talking to Ellen. Why this new superfluous caring?

I want for them not to have died in awful pain, friendless.
Though many of the living are starving, I still pray for these,

Dead, mostly anonymous (but Mr. Monk, Mrs. Rose Vogel)
And barely remembered: that they had a little extra, something

For pleasure, a good meal, a book or a decent television set.
Of whom do I pray this rubbery, low-class charity? I saw

An expert today, a nun—wearing a regular skirt and blouse,
But the hood or headdress navy and white around her plain

Probably Irish face, older than me by five or ten years.
The Post Office clerk told her he couldn't break a twenty

So she got change next door and came back to send her package.
As I came out she was driving off—with an air, it seemed to me,

Of annoying, demure good cheer, as if the reasonableness
Of change, mail, cars, clothes was a pleasure in itself: veiled

And dumb like the girls I thought enjoyed the rules too much
In grade school. She might have been a grade school teacher;

But she reminded me of being there, aside from that—as a name
And person there, a Mary or John who learns that the janitor

Is Mr. Woodhouse; the principal is Mr. Ringleven; the secretary
In the office is Mrs. Apostolacos; the bus driver is Ray.

DYING

Nothing to be said about it, and everything—
The change of changes, closer or farther away:
The Golden Retriever next door, Gussie, is dead,

Like Sandy, the Cocker Spaniel from three doors down
Who died when I was small; and every day
Things that were in my memory fade and die.

Phrases die out: first, everyone forgets
What doornails are; then after certain decades
As a dead metaphor, *"dead as a doornail"* flickers

And fades away. But someone I know is dying—
And though one might say glibly, "everyone is,"
The different pace makes the difference absolute.

The tiny invisible spores in the air we breathe,
That settle harmlessly on our drinking water
And on our skin, happen to come together

With certain conditions on the forest floor,
Or even a shady corner of the lawn—
And overnight the fleshy, pale stalks gather,

The colorless growth without a leaf or flower;
And around the stalks, the summer grass keeps growing
With steady pressure, like the insistent whiskers

That grow between shaves on a face, the nails
Growing and dying from the toes and fingers
At their own humble pace, oblivious

As the nerveless moths, that live their night or two—
Though like a moth a bright soul keeps on beating,
Bored and impatient in the monster's mouth.

THE GARDEN

Far back, in the most remote times with their fresh colors,
Already and without knowing it I must have begun to bring
Everyone into the shadowy garden—half-overgrown,

A kind of lush, institutional grounds—
Singly or in groups, into that green recess. Everything
Is muffled there; they walk over a rich mulch

Where I have conducted them together into summer shade
And go on bringing them, all arriving with no more commotion
Than the intermittent rustling of birds in the dense leaves,

Or birds' notes in chains or knots that embroider
The sleek sounds of water bulging over the dam's brim:
Midafternoon voices of chickadee, kingbird, catbird;

And the falls, hung in a cool, thick nearly motionless sheet
From the little green pond to shatter perpetually in mist
Over the streambed. And like statuary of dark metal

Or pale stone around the pond, the living and the dead,
Young and old, gather where they are brought: some nameless;
Some victims and some brazen conquerors; the shamed; the haunters;

The harrowed; the cherished; the banished—or background figures,
Old men from a bench, girl with glasses from school—brought beyond
Even memory's noises and rages, here in the quiet garden.

THE NEW SADDHUS

Barefoot, in unaccustomed clouts or skirts of raw muslin,
With new tin cup, rattle or scroll held in diffident hands
Stripped of the familiar cuffs, rings, watches, the new holy-men

Avoid looking at their farewelling families, an elaborate
Feigned concentration stretched over their self-consciousness and terror,
Like small boys nervous on the first day of baseball tryouts.

Fearful exalted Coptic tradesman; Swedish trucker; Palestinian doctor;
The Irish works foreman and the Lutheran Optometrist from St. Paul:
They line up smirking or scowling, feeling silly, determined,

All putting aside the finite piercing recklessness of men
Who in this world have provided for their generation: O they have
Swallowed their wives' girlhoods and their children's dentistry,

Dowries and tuitions. And grown fat with swallowing they line up
Endless as the Ganges or the piles of old newspapers at the dumps,
Which may be blankets for them now; intense and bathetic

As the founders of lodges, they will overcome fatigue, self-pity, desire,
O Lords of mystery, to stare endlessly at the sun till the last
Red retinal ghost of actual sight is burned utterly away,

And still turn eyes that see no more than the forehead can see
Daily and all day toward the first faint heat of the morning.
Ready O Lords to carry one kilo of sand more each month,

More weight and more, so the fabulous thick mortified muscles
Lurch and bulge under an impossible tonnage of stupid,
Particulate inertia, and still O Lords ready, men and not women

And not young men, but the respectable Kurd, Celt, Marxist
And Rotarian, chanting and shuffling in place a little now
Like their own pimply, reformed-addict children, as they put aside

The garb, gear, manners and bottomless desires of their completed
Responsibilities; they are a shambles of a comic drill-team
But holy, holy—holy, becoming their own animate worshipful

Soon all but genderless flesh, a cooked sanctified recklessness—
O the old marks of elastic, leather, metal razors, callousing tools,
Pack straps and belts, fading from their embarrassed bodies!

THE STREET

Streaked and fretted with effort, the thick
Vine of the world, red nervelets
Coiled at its tips.

All roads lead from it. All night
Wainwrights and upholsterers work finishing
The wheeled coffin

Of the dead favorite of the Emperor,
The child's corpse propped seated
On brocade, with yellow

Oiled curls, kohl on the stiff lids.
Slaves throw petals on the roadway
For the cortege, white

Languid flowers shooting from dark
Blisters on the vine, ramifying
Into streets. On mine,

Rockwell Avenue, it was embarrassing:
Trouble—fights, the police, sickness—
Seemed never to come

For anyone when they were fully dressed.
It was always underwear or dirty pajamas,
Unseemly stretches

Of skin showing through a torn housecoat.
Once a stranger drove off in a car
With somebody's wife,

And he ran after them in his undershirt
And threw his shoe at the car. It bounced
Into the street

Harmlessly, and we carried it back to him;
But the man had too much dignity
To put it back on,

So he held it and stood crying in the street:
"He's breaking up my home," he said,
"The son of a bitch

Bastard is breaking up my home." The street
Rose undulant in pavement-breaking coils
And the man rode it,

Still holding his shoe and stiffly upright
Like a trick rider in the circus parade
That came down the street

Each August. As the powerful dragonlike
Hump swelled he rose cursing and ready
To throw his shoe—woven

Angular as a twig into the fabulous
Rug or brocade with crowns and camels,
Leopards and rosettes,

All riding the vegetable wave of the street
From the John Flock Mortuary Home
Down to the river.

It was a small place, and off the center,
But so much a place to itself, I felt
Like a young prince

Or aspirant squire. I knew that *Ivanhoe*
Was about race. The Saxons were Jews,
Or even Coloreds,

With their low-ceilinged, unbelievably
Sour-smelling houses down by the docks.
Everything was written

Or woven, ivory and pink and emerald—
Nothing was too ugly or petty or terrible
To be weighed in the immense

Silver scales of the dead: the looming
Balances set right onto the live, dangerous
Gray bark of the street.

FROM

AN EXPLANATION OF AMERICA

1979

LAIR

Inexhaustible, delicate, as if
Without source or medium, daylight
Undoes the mind; the infinite,

Empty actual is too bright,
Scattering to where the road
Whispers, through a mile of woods . . .

Later, how quiet the house is:
Dusk-like and refined,
The sweet Phoebe-note

Piercing from the trees;
The calm globe of the morning,
Things to read or to write

Ranged on a table: the brain
A dark, stubborn current that breathes
Blood, a deaf wadding,

The hands feeding it paper
And sensations of wood or metal
On its own terms. Trying to read

I persist awhile, finish the recognition
By my breath of a dead giant's breath —
Stayed by the space of a rhythm,

Witnessing the blue gulf of the air.

(A Poem to My Daughter)

PART TWO, I. *A Love of Death*

Imagine a child from Virginia or New Hampshire
Alone on the prairie eighty years ago
Or more, one afternoon — the shaggy pelt
Of grasses, for the first time in that child's life,
Flowing for miles. Imagine the moving shadow
Of a cloud far off across that shadeless ocean,
The obliterating strangeness like a tide
That pulls or empties the bubble of the child's
Imaginary heart. No hills, no trees.

The child's heart lightens, tending like a bubble
Towards the currents of the grass and sky,
The pure potential of the clear blank spaces.

Or, imagine the child in a draw that holds a garden
Cupped from the limitless motion of the prairie,
Head resting against a pumpkin, in evening sun.
Ground-cherry bushes grow along the furrows,

The fruit red under its papery, moth-shaped sheath.
Grasshoppers tumble among the vines, as large
As dragons in the crumbs of pale dry earth.
The ground is warm to the child's cheek, and the wind
Is a humming sound in the grass above the draw,
Rippling the shadows of the red-green blades.
The bubble of the child's heart melts a little,
Because the quiet of that air and earth
Is like the shadow of a peaceful death—
Limitless and potential; a kind of space
Where one dissolves to become a part of something
Entire . . . whether of sun and air, or goodness
And knowledge, it does not matter to the child.

Dissolved among the particles of the garden
Or into the motion of the grass and air,
Imagine the child happy to be a thing.

Imagine, then, that on that same wide prairie
Some people are threshing in the terrible heat
With horses and machines, cutting bands
And shoveling amid the clatter of the threshers,
The chaff in prickly clouds and the naked sun
Burning as if it could set the chaff on fire.
Imagine that the people are Swedes or Germans,
Some of them resting pressed against the strawstacks,
Trying to get the meager shade.
                                    A man,
A tramp, comes laboring across the stubble
Like a mirage against that blank horizon,

Laboring in his torn shoes toward the tall
Mirage-like images of the tilted threshers
Clattering in the heat. Because the Swedes
Or Germans have no beer, or else because
They cannot speak his language properly,
Or for some reason one cannot imagine,
The man climbs up on a thresher and cuts bands
A minute or two, then waves to one of the people,
A young girl or a child, and jumps head-first
Into the sucking mouth of the machine,
Where he is wedged and beat and cut to pieces—
While the people shout and run in the clouds of chaff,
Like lost mirages on the pelt of prairie.

The poet Horace, writing to a friend
About his Sabine farm and other matters,
Implies his answer about aspiration
Within the prison of empire or republic:

"Dear Quinctius:
                    I'll tell you a little about
My farm—in case you ever happen to wonder
About the place: as, what I make in grain,
Or if I'm getting rich on olives, apples,
Timber or pasture.
                    There are hills, unbroken
Except for one soft valley, cut at an angle
That sweetens the climate, because it takes the sun
All morning on its right slope, until the left
Has its turn, warming as the sun drives past
All afternoon. You'd like it here: the plums
And low-bush berries are ripe; and where my cows
Fill up on acorns and ilex-berries a lush
Canopy of shade gives pleasure to their master.
The green is deep, so deep you'd say Tarentum
Had somehow nestled closer, to be near Rome.

There is a spring, fit for a famous river
(The Hebrus winds through Thrace no colder or purer),

Useful for healing stomach-aches and head-aches.
And here I keep myself, and the place keeps me —
A precious good, believe it, Quinctius —
In health and sweetness through September's heat.

You of course live in the way that is truly right,
If you've been careful to remain the man
That we all see in you. We here in Rome
Talk of you, always, as 'happy' . . . there is the fear,
Of course, that one might listen too much to others,
Think what they see, and strive to be that thing,
And lose by slow degrees that inward man
Others first noticed — as though, if over and over
Everyone tells you you're in marvelous health,
You might towards dinner-time, when a latent fever
Falls on you, try for a long while to disguise it,
Until the trembling rattles your food-smeared hands.
It's foolishness to camouflage our sores.

Take 'recognition' — what if someone writes
A speech about your service to your country,
Telling for your attentive ears the roll
Of all your victories by land or sea,
With choice quotations, dignified periods,
And skillful terms, all in the second person,
As in the citations for honorary degrees;
'Only a mind beyond our human powers
Could judge if your great love for Rome exceeds,
Or is exceeded by, Rome's need for you.'

—You'd find it thrilling, but inappropriate
For anyone alive, except Augustus.

And yet if someone calls me 'wise' or 'flawless'
Must one protest? I like to be told I'm right,
And brilliant, as much as any other man.
The trouble is, the people who give out
The recognition, compliments, degrees
Can take them back tomorrow, if they choose:
Sorry, but isn't that ours, that you nearly took?
What can I do, but shuffle sadly off?
If the same people scream that I'm a crook
Who'd strangle my father for money to buy a drink,
Should I turn white with pain and humiliation?
If prizes and insults from outside have much power
To hurt or give joy, something is sick inside.

Who is the good man?
                              Many people would answer,
'He is the man who never breaks the law
Or violates our codes. His judgment is sound.
He is the man whose word is as his bond.
If such a man agrees to be your witness,
Your case is won.'
                              And yet this very man,
If you ask his family, or the people who know him,
Is like a rotten egg in its flawless shell.
And if a slave or prisoner should say
'I never steal, I never try to escape,'

My answer is, 'You have your just rewards:
No beatings; no solitary; and your food.'

'I have not killed.' 'You won't be crucified.'
'But haven't I shown that I am good, and honest?'

To this, my country neighbor would shake his head
And sigh: 'Ah no! The wolf himself is wary
Because he fears the pit, as hawks the snare
Or pike the hook. Some folk hate vice for love
Of the good: you're merely afraid of guards and crosses.'

Apply that peasant wisdom to that 'good man'
Of forum and tribunal, who in the temple
Calls loudly on 'Father Janus' or 'Apollo'
But in an undertone implores, 'Laverna,
Goddess of thieves, O Fair One, grant me, please,
That I get away with it, let me pass as upright,
Cover my sins with darkness, my lies with clouds.'

When a man stoops to pluck at the coin some boys
Of Rome have soldered to the street, I think
That just then he is no more free than any
Prisoner or slave; it seems that someone who wants
Too much to get things is also someone who fears,
And living in that fear cannot be free.
A man has thrown away his weapons, has quit
The struggle for virtue, who is always busy
Filling his wants, getting things, making hay—
Weaponless and defenseless as a captive.

When you have got a captive, you never kill him
If you can sell him for a slave; this man
Truly will make a good slave: persevering,
Ambitious, eager to please—as plowman, or shepherd,
Or trader plying your goods at sea all winter,
Or helping to carry fodder on the farm . . .
The truly good, and wise man has more courage,
And if need be, will find the freedom to say,
As in the *Bacchae* of Euripides:

King Pentheus, King of Thebes, what will you force me
To suffer at your hands?
                              I will take your goods.

You mean my cattle, furniture, cloth and plate?
Then you may have them.
                              I will put you, chained,
Into my prison, under a cruel guard.

Then God himself, the moment that I choose,
Will set me free . . .

I think that what this means is, 'I will die.'

Death is the chalk-line toward which all things race."

PART TWO, IV. *Filling the Blank*

Odd, that the poet who seems so complacent
About his acorns and his cold pure water,
Writing from his retreat just out of Rome,
Should seem to end with a different love of death
From that of someone on a mystic plain —
But still, with love of death. ". . . A rather short man,"
He calls himself, "and prematurely gray,
Who liked to sit in the sun; a freedman's child
Who spread his wings too wide for that frail nest
And yet found favor, in both war and peace,
With powerful men. Tell them I lost my temper
Easily, but was easily appeased,
My book — and if they chance to ask my age
Say, I completed my forty-fourth December
In the first year that Lepidus was Consul."

I think that what the poet meant was this:
That freedom, even in a free Republic,
Rests ultimately on the right to die.
And though he's careful to say that Quinctius,
The public man able to act for good
And help his fellow-Romans, lives the life
That truly is the best, he's also careful
To separate their fortunes and their places,
And to appreciate his own: his health,

His cows and acorns and his healing spring,
His circle—"*We here in Rome*"—for friends and gossip.

It would be too complacent to build a nest
Between one's fatalism and one's pleasures—
With death at one side, a sweet farm at the other,
Keeping the thorns of government away . . .

Horace's father, who had been a slave,
Engaged in some small business near Venusia;
And like a Jewish or Armenian merchant
Who does well in America, he sent
His son to Rome's best schools, and then to Athens
(It's hard to keep from thinking "as to Harvard")
To study, with the sons of gentlemen
And politicians, the higher arts most useful
To citizens of a Republic: math;
Philosophy; rhetoric in all its branches.

One March, when Horace, not quite twenty-one,
Was still at Athens, Julius Caesar died,
And the Roman world was split by civil war.

When Brutus came to Athens late that summer
On his way to Asia Minor—"half-mystical,
Wholly romantic Brutus"—Horace quit school
To follow Brutus to Asia, bearing the title
Or brevet-commission tribunus militum,
And served on the staff of the patriot-assassin.

Time passed; the father died; the property
And business were lost, or confiscated.
The son saw action at Philippi, where,
Along with other enthusiastic students
(Cicero's son among them), and tens of thousands
In the two largest armies of Roman soldiers
Ever to fight with one another, he shared
In the republican army's final rout
By Antony and Octavian.
                              Plutarch says
That Brutus, just before he killed himself,
Speaking in Greek to an old fellow-student,
Said that although he was angry for his country
He was deeply happy for himself—because
His virtue and his repute for virtue were founded
In a way none of the conquerors could hope,
For all their arms and riches, to emulate;
Nor could they hinder posterity from knowing,
And saying, that they were unjust and wicked men
Who had destroyed justice and the Republic,
Usurping a power to which they had no right.

The corpse of Brutus was found by Antony,
And he commanded the richest purple mantle
In his possession to be thrown over it,
And afterward, the mantle being stolen,
He found the thief and had him put to death;
The ashes of Brutus he sent back to Rome,
To be received with honor by the mourners.

Horace came back to Rome a pardoned rebel
In his late twenties, without cash or prospects,
Having stretched out his wings too far beyond
The frail nest of his freedman father's hopes,
As he has written.
                        When he was thirty-five,
He published some poems which some people praised,
And so through Virgil he met the Roman knight
And good friend of Augustus, called Maecenas,
Who befriended him, and gave him the Sabine farm;
And in that place, and in the highest circles
In Rome itself, he spent his time, and wrote.

Since aspirations need not (some say, should not)
Be likely, should I wish for you to be
A hero, like Brutus—who at the finish-line
Declared himself to be a happy man?
Or is the right wish health, the just proportion
Of sun, the acorns and cold pure water, a nest
Out in the country and a place in Rome . . .

Of course, one's aspirations must depend
Upon the opportunities: the justice
That happens to be available; one's fortune.
I think that what the poet meant may be
Something like that; and as for aspiration,
Maybe our aspirations for ourselves
Ought to be different from the hopes we have
(Though there are warnings against too much hope)
When thinking of our children. And in fact
Our fantasies about the perfect life

Are different for ourselves and for our children,
Theirs being safer, less exciting, purer—
And so, depending always on the chances
Our country offers, it seems we should aspire,
For ourselves, to struggle actively to save
The Republic—or to be, if not like Brutus,
Like Quinctius: a citizen of affairs,
Free in the state and in the love of death . . .
While for our children we are bound to aspire
Differently: something like a nest or farm;
So that the cycle of different aspirations
Threads through posterity.
                                        And who can say
What Brutus may come sweeping through your twenties—
Given the taste you have for noble speeches,
For causes lost and glamorous and just.

Did Horace's father, with his middle-class
And slavish aspirations, have it right?—
To give your child the education fit
For the upper classes: math, philosophy,
And rhetoric in all its branches; so I
Must want for you, when you must fall upon
The sword of government or mortality—
Since all of us, even you, race toward it—to have
The power to make your parting speech in Greek
(Or in the best equivalent) and if
You ever write for fame or money, that Virgil
Will pick your book out from a hundred others,
If that's not plucking at a soldered coin.

PART THREE, I. *Braveries*

Once, while a famous town lay torn and burning
A woman came to childbed, and lay in labor
While all around her people cursed and screamed
In desperation, and soldiers raged insanely—
So that the child came out, the story says,
In the loud center of every horror of war.
And looking on that scene, just halfway out,
The child retreated backward, to the womb:
And chose to make those quiet walls its urn.

"Brave infant of Saguntum," a poet says—
As though to embrace a limit might show courage.
(Although the word is more like *bravo*, the glory
Of a great tenor, the swagger of new clothes:
The infant as a brilliant moral performer
Defying in its retreat the bounds of life.)
Denial of limit has been the pride, or failing,
Famously shared by all our country's regions,
Races, and classes, as though prepared to challenge
The idea of sufficiency itself . . .
And while it seems that in the name of limit
Some people are choosing to have fewer children,
Or none, that too can be a gesture of freedom—
A way to deny or brave the bounds of time.

A boundary is a limit. How can I
Describe for you the boundaries of this place
Where we were born: where Possibility spreads
And multiplies and exhausts itself in growing,
And opens yawning to swallow itself again,
Unrealized horizons forever dissolving?

A field house built of corrugated metal,
The frosted windows tilted open inward
In two lines high along the metal walls;
Inside, a horse-ring and a horse called Yankee
Jogging around the ring with clouds of dust
Rising and settling in the still, cold air
Behind the horse and rider as they course
Rhythmically through the bars of washed-out light
That fall in dim arcades all down the building.

The rider, a girl of seven or eight called Rose,
Concentrates firmly on her art, her body,
Her small, straight back and shoulders as they rise
Together with the alternate, gray shoulders
Of the unweary horse. Her father stands
And watches, in a business suit and coat,
Watching the child's face under the black serge helmet,
Her yellow hair that bounces at her nape
And part-way down her back. He feels the cold
Of the dry, sunless earth up through the soles
Of his thin, inappropriate dress shoes.

He feels the limit of that simple cold,
And braves it, concentrating on the progress
Of the child riding in circles around the ring.
She is so charming that he feels less mortal.
As from the bravery of a fancy suit,
He takes crude courage from the ancient meaning
Of the horse, as from a big car or a business:
He feels as if the world had fewer limits.
The primitive symbols of the horse and girl
Seem goods profound and infinite, as clear
As why the stuffs of merchants are called, "goods."

The goods of all the world seem possible
And clear in that brave spectacle, the rise
Up from the earth and onto the property
Of horses and the history of riding.
In his vague yearning, as he muses on goods
Lost and confused as chivalry, he might
Dream anything: as from the Cavalier
One might dream up the Rodeo, or the Ford,
Or some new thing the country waited for—
Some property, some consuming peasant dream
Of horses and walls; as though the Rodeo
And Ford were elegiac gestures; as though
Invented things gave birth to long-lost goods.

The country, boasting that it cannot see
The past, waits dreaming ever of the past,
Or all the plural pasts: the way a fetus
Dreams vaguely of heaven—waiting, and in its courage

Willing, not only to be born out into
The Actual (with its ambiguous goods),
But to retreat again and be born backwards
Into the gallant walls of its potential,
Its sheltered circle . . . willing to leave behind,
It might be, carnage.
                              What shall we keep open —
Where shall we throw our courage, where retreat?

White settlers disembarked here, to embark
Upon a mountain-top of huge potential —
Which for the disembarking slaves was low:
A swamp, or valley of dry bones, where they lay
In labor with a brilliant, strange slave-culture —
All emigrants, ever disembarking. *Shall these*
Bones live? And in a jangle of confusion
And hunger, from the mountains to the valleys,
They rise; and breathe; and fall in the wind again.

MEMORIAL

(J.E. and N.M.S.)

Here lies a man. And here, a girl. They live
In the kind of artificial life we give

To birds or statues: imagining what they feel,
Or that like birds the dead each had one call,

Repeated, or a gesture that suspends
Their being in a forehead or the hands.

A man comes whistling from a house. The screen
Snaps shut behind him. Though there is no man

And no house, memory sends him to get tools
From a familiar shed, and so he strolls

Through summer shade to work on the family car.
He is my uncle, and fresh home from the war

With nothing for me to remember him doing yet.
The clock of the cancer ticks in his body, or not,

Depending if it is there, or waits. The search
Of memory gains and fails like surf: the porch

And trim are painted cream, the shakes are stained.
The shadows could be painted (so little wind

Is blowing there) or stains on the crazy-paving
Of the front walk ... Or now, the shadows are moving:

Another house, unrelated; a woman says,
Is this your special boy, and the girl says, yes,

Moving her hand in mine. The clock in her, too—
As someone told me a month or two ago,

Months after it finally took her. A public building
Is where the house was: though a surf, unyielding

And sickly, seethes and eddies at the stones
Of the foundation. The dead are made of bronze,

But living they were like birds with clocklike hearts—
Unthinkable how much pain the tiny parts

Of even the smallest bird might yet contain.
We become larger than life in how much pain

Our bodies may encompass ... all Titans in that,
Or heroic statues. Although there is no heat

Brimming in the fixed, memorial summer, the brows
Of lucid metals sweat a faint warm haze

As I try to think the pain I never saw.
Though there is no pain there, the small birds draw

Together in crowds above the houses—and cry
Over the surf: as if there were a day,

Memorial, marked on the calendar for dread
And pain and loss—although among the dead

Are no hurts, but only emblematic things;
No hospital beds, but a lifting of metal wings.

FROM

SADNESS AND HAPPINESS

1975

POEM ABOUT PEOPLE

The jaunty crop-haired graying
Women in grocery stores,
Their clothes boyish and neat,
New mittens or clean sneakers,

Clean hands, hips not bad still,
Buying ice cream, steaks, soda,
Fresh melons and soap—or the big
Balding young men in work shoes

And green work pants, beer belly
And white T-shirt, the porky walk
Back to the truck, polite; possible
To feel briefly like Jesus,

A gust of diffuse tenderness
Crossing the dark spaces
To where the dry self burrows
Or nests, something that stirs,

Watching the kinds of people
On the street for a while—
But how love falters and flags
When anyone's difficult eyes come

Into focus, terrible gaze of a unique
Soul, its need unlovable: my friend
In his divorced schoolteacher
Apartment, his own unsuspected

Paintings hung everywhere,
Which his wife kept in a closet—
Not, he says, that she wasn't
Perfectly right; or me, mis-hearing

My rock radio sing my self-pity:
"The Angels Wished Him Dead"—all
The hideous, sudden stare of self,
Soul showing through like the lizard

Ancestry showing in the frontal gaze
Of a robin busy on the lawn.
In the movies, when the sensitive
Young Jewish soldier nearly drowns

Trying to rescue the thrashing
Anti-Semitic bully, swimming across
The river raked by nazi fire,
The awful part is the part truth:

Hate my whole kind, but me,
Love me for myself. The weather
Changes in the black of night,
And the dream-wind, bowling across

The sopping open spaces
Of roads, golf courses, parking lots,
Flails a commotion
In the dripping treetops,

Tries a half-rotten shingle
Or a down-hung branch, and we
All dream it, the dark wind crossing
The wide spaces between us.

FROM AN ESSAY ON

PSYCHIATRISTS

XX. PERORATION,

CONCERNING GENIUS

Odd that so many writers, makers of films,
Artists, all suitors of excellence consult
Psychiatrists, willing to risk that therapy, easing

The anguish, might smooth away the cicatrice
Of genius, too. But it is all bosh, the false
Link between genius and sickness,

Except perhaps as they were linked
By the Old Man, addressing his class
On the first day: *"I know why you are here.*

You are here to laugh. You have heard of a crazy
Old man who believes that Robert Bridges
Was a good poet; who believes that Fulke

Greville was a great poet, greater than Philip
Sidney; who believes that Shakespeare's Sonnets
Are not all that they are cracked up to be ... Well,

I will tell you something: I will tell you
What this course is about. Sometime in the middle
Of the Eighteenth Century, along with the rise

Of capitalism and scientific method, the logical
Foundations of Western thought decayed and fell apart.
When they fell apart, poets were left

With emotions and experiences, and with no way
To examine them. At this time, poets and men
Of genius began to go mad. Gray went mad. Collins

Went mad. Kit Smart was mad. William Blake surely
Was a madman. Coleridge was a drug addict, with severe
Depression. My friend Hart Crane died mad. My friend

Ezra Pound is mad. But you will not go mad; you will grow up
To become happy, sentimental old college professors,
Because they were men of genius, and you

Are not; and the ideas which were vital
To them are mere amusement to you. I will not
Go mad, because I have understood those ideas ..."

He drank wine and smoked his pipe more than he should;
In the end his doctors in order to prolong life
Were forced to cut away most of his tongue.

That was their business. As far as he was concerned
Suffering was life's penalty; wisdom armed one
Against madness; speech was temporary; poetry was truth.

FIRST EARLY

MORNINGS TOGETHER

Waking up over the candy store together
We hear the birds waking up below the sill
And slowly recognize ourselves, the weather,
The time, and the birds that rustle there until

Down to the street as fog and silence lift
The pigeons from the wrinkled awning flutter
To reconnoiter, mutter, stare and shift
Pecking by ones or twos the rainbowed gutter.

SADNESS AND HAPPINESS

I

That they have no earthly measure
is well known—the surprise is
how often it becomes impossible
to tell one from the other in memory:

the sadness of past failures, the strangely
happy—doubtless corrupt—
fondling of them. Crude, empty
though the terms are, they do

organize life: sad American house-
hunting couples with kids
and small savings visit Model Homes each
Sunday for years; humble,

they need closet space, closet
space to organize life . . . in older countries
people seem to be happy with less closet
space. Empty space,

I suppose, also explains *post
coitum triste*, a phenomenon
which on reflection I am happy
to find rare in my memory—not,

II

God knows, that sex isn't crucial, a
desire to get more or better
must underlie the "pain" and "bliss"
of sonnets—or is it a need to *do* better:

A girl touched my sleeve, once,
held it, deep-eyed; life too at times
has come up, looked into my face,
My Lord, how like you this? And I?

Always distracted by some secret
movie camera or absurd audience
eager for clichés, *Ivanhoe*, de blues,
Young Man with a Horn, the star

tripping over his lance, quill, phallic
symbol or saxophone—miserable,
these absurd memories of failure
to see anything but oneself,

my pride, my consciousness, my shame, my
sickly haze of Romance—sick too
the root of joy? "Bale" and "bliss" merge
in a Petrarchist grin, that sleeve's burden

III

or chivalric trophy to bear as
emblem or mark of the holy
idiot: know ye, this natural stood
posing amiss while the best prizes

of life bounced off his vague
pate or streamed between his legs—
did Korsh, Old Russia's bedlam-sage,
enjoy having princesses visit his cell?

Would they dote on me as I shake out
a match, my fountain pen in the same
hand, freckling my dim brow with ink?
Into his muttered babble they read tips

on the market, court, marriage—I too
mutter: *Fool, fool!* or *Death!*
or *Joy!* Well, somewhere in the mind's mess
feelings are genuine, someone's

mad voice undistracted, clarity
maybe of motive and precise need
like an enameled sky, cool
blue of Indian Summer, happiness

I V

like the sex-drowsy saxophones
rolling flatted thirds of the blues
over and over, rocking the dulcet
rhythms of regret, Black music

which tumbles loss over in the mouth
like a moist bone full of marrow;
the converse is a good mood grown
too rich, like dark water steeping

willow roots in the shade, spotted
with sun and slight odor of dirt
or death, insane quibbles of self-
regard . . . better to mutter *fool*

or feel solaces of unmerited
Grace, like a road of inexplicable
dells, rises and lakes, found
in a flat place of no lakes — or feel

the senses: cheese, bread, tart
apples and wine, broiling acres
of sunflowers in Spain, mansards
in Vermont, painted shay and pard,

v

or the things I see, driving
with you: houses and cars, trees,
grasses and birds; people, incidents
of the senses—like women and men, dusk

on a golf course, waving clubs
dreamily in slow practice-gestures
profiled against a sky layered
purplish turquoise and gray, having

sport in the evening; or white
selvage of a mockingbird's gray
blur as he dabbles wings and tail
in a gutter—all in a way fraught,

full of emotion, and yet empty—
how can I say it?—all empty
of sadness and happiness, deep
blank passions, waiting like houses

and cars of a strange place,
a profound emptiness that came once
in the car, your cheekbone, lashes,
hair at my vision's edge, driving

VI

back from Vermont and then
into the iron dusk of Cambridge,
Central Square suddenly become
the most strange of places

as a Salvation Army band marches
down the middle, shouldering aside
the farting, evil-tempered traffic,
brass pitting its triplets and sixteenths

into the sundown fray of cops, gesturing
derelicts, young girls begging quarters,
shoppers and released secretaries, scruffy
workers and students, dropouts, children

whistling, gathering as the band
steps in place tootling and rumbling
in the square now, under an apocalypse
of green-and-pink sky, with paper

and filth spinning in the wind, crazy,
everyone — band, audience, city, lady
trumpeter fiddling spit-valve, John
Philip Sousa, me, Christianity, crazy

VII

and all empty except for you,
who look sometimes like a stranger;
as a favorite room, lake, picture
might look seen after years away,

your face at a new angle grows
unfamiliar and blank, love's face
perhaps, where I chose once to dream
again, but better, those past failures —

"Some lovely, glorious Nothing," Susan,
Patricia, Celia, forgive me — God,
a girl in my street was called Half-
A-Buck, not right in her head . . .

how happy I would be, or else
decently sad, with no past: you
only and no foolish ghosts
urging me to become some redeeming

Jewish-American Shakespeare
(or God knows what they expect,
Longfellow) and so excuse my thorny
egotism, my hard-ons of self-concern,

VIII

melodramas and speeches
of myself, crazy in love with
my status as a sad young man: dreams
of myself old, a vomit-stained

ex-jazz-Immortal, collapsed
in a phlegmy Bowery doorway
on Old Mr. Boston lemon-flavored
gin or on cheap wine—that romantic

fantasy of my future bumhood
excused all manner of lies, fumbles,
destructions, even this minute, "*Mea
culpa!*" I want to scream, stealing

the podium to address the band,
the kids, the old ladies awaiting
buses, the glazed winos (who accomplished
my dream while I got you, and art,

and daughters); "Oh you city of
undone deathcrotches! Terrible
the film of green brainpus! Fog
of corruption at the great shitfry! No

IX

grease-trickling sink
of disorder in your depressed
avenues is more terrible
than these, and not your whole

aggregate of pollution
is more heavy than the measure
of unplumbed muttering
remorse, shame, inchoate pride

and nostalgia in any one
sulphur-choked, grit-breathing
citizen of the place ..." Sad,
the way one in part enjoys

air pollution, relishes
millennial doom, headlines,
even the troubles of friends —
or, OK, enjoys hearing

and talking about them, anyway—
to be whole-hearted is rare;
changing as the heart does, is it
the heart, or the sun emerging from

x

or going behind a cloud,
or a change somewhere in my eyes?
Terrible, to think that mere pretty
scenery—or less, the heraldic shape

of an oak leaf drifting down
curbside waters in the sun, pink
bittersweet among the few last
gray sad leaves of the fall—can bring

joy, or fail to. Shouldn't I vow
to seek only within myself
my only hire? Or not? All my senses,
like beacon's flame, counsel gratitude

for the two bright-faced girls
crossing the Square, beauty a light
or intelligence, no quarters for them,
long legs flashing bravely above

the grime—it is as if men were to
go forth plumed in white
uniforms and swords; how could we
ever aspire to such smartness,

XI

such happy grace? Pretty enough
plumage and all, a man in the bullshit
eloquence of his sad praises stumbles,
fumbles: *fool.* It is true, wonder

does indeed hinder love and hate,
and one can behold well with eyes
only what lies beneath him—
so that it takes more than eyes

to see well anything that is worth
loving; that is the sad part, the senses
are not visionary, they can tug
downward, even in pure joy—

trivial joy, the deep solid crack
of the bat. A sandlot home run
has led me to clown circling
the diamond as though cheered

by a make-believe audience
of thousands (you, dead poets, friends,
old coaches and teachers, everyone
I ever knew) cheering louder as I tip

XII

my imaginary, ironic hat and blow
false kisses crossing home, happiness
impure and oddly memorable as the sad
agony of recalled errors lived over

before sleep, poor throws awry
or the ball streaming through,
between my poor foolish legs, crouching
amazëd like a sot. Sport—woodmanship,

ball games, court games—has its cruel
finitude of skill, good-and-bad, as does
the bizarre art of words: confirmation
of a good word, *polvo*, dust, reddish gray

powder of the ballfield, *el polvo*
rising in pale puffs to glaze lightly
the brown ankles and brown bare feet in
Cervantes' poem of the girl dancing, all

dust now, poet, girl. It is intolerable
to think of my daughters, too, dust—
el polvo—you whose invented game,
Sadness and Happiness, soothes them

XIII

to sleep: can you tell me one sad
thing that happened today, Can you think
of one happy thing to tell me that
happened to you today, organizing

life — not you too dust like the poets,
dancers, athletes, their dear skills
and the alleged glittering gaiety of
Art which, in my crabwise scribbling hand,

no less than Earth the change of all
changes breedeth, art and life
both inconstant mothers, in whose
fixed cold bosoms we lie fixed,

desperate to devise anything, any
sadness or happiness, only
to escape the clasped coffinworm
truth of eternal art or marmoreal

infinite nature, twin stiff
destined measures both manifested
by my shoes, coated with dust or dew which no
earthly measure will survive.

NOTES

"Song on Porcelain" and "Incantation" are based on unpublished English trots provided by Czeslaw Milosz. ("Song on Porcelain" deliberately changes Milosz's refrain.) My rhymed "An Old Man" is based on published English versions of Constantine Cavafy's poem, notably the one in Edmund Keeley and Philip Sherrard's *Collected Poems*. In a similar way, "Akhmatova's Summer Garden" is indebted to Akhmatova translations, including the excellent one by Judith Hemschemeyer. "Samurai Song" imitates an ancient Japanese model, or various renderings of it.

The selection from "An Explanation of America" follows the Latin of Horace's epistle as closely as I can, except for a few anachronisms like the reference to honorary degrees.

Parts of "Shirt" versify a much-quoted—and possibly fabricated—newspaper account attributed to "a witness" of the Triangle Shirtwaist Factory fire; the scene of the young man dropping the young women, then leaping to his own death, is in the realm of things that might or might not have happened. "Love of Death" borrows phrases and images from Willa Cather's *My Antonia*.

In "Louie Louie," "Numerus Clausus" is the traditional term for a quota limiting the number of Jews admitted to universities: first at schools in Poland and Russia and then later—into the nineteen sixties—at "elite" American private universities. The story is told most recently in Jerome Karabel's 2005 book, *The Chosen: The Hidden History of Admission and Exclusion at Harvard, Yale, and Princeton*. In "The Forgetting," Sibby Sisti (though some readers have mistaken his name for a Latin phrase) played shortstop and second base for the Boston Braves in the early nineteen fifties.

R.P.